Peter Halley

Peter Halley

Boats Crosses Trees Figures
Gouaches 1977–78

Karma

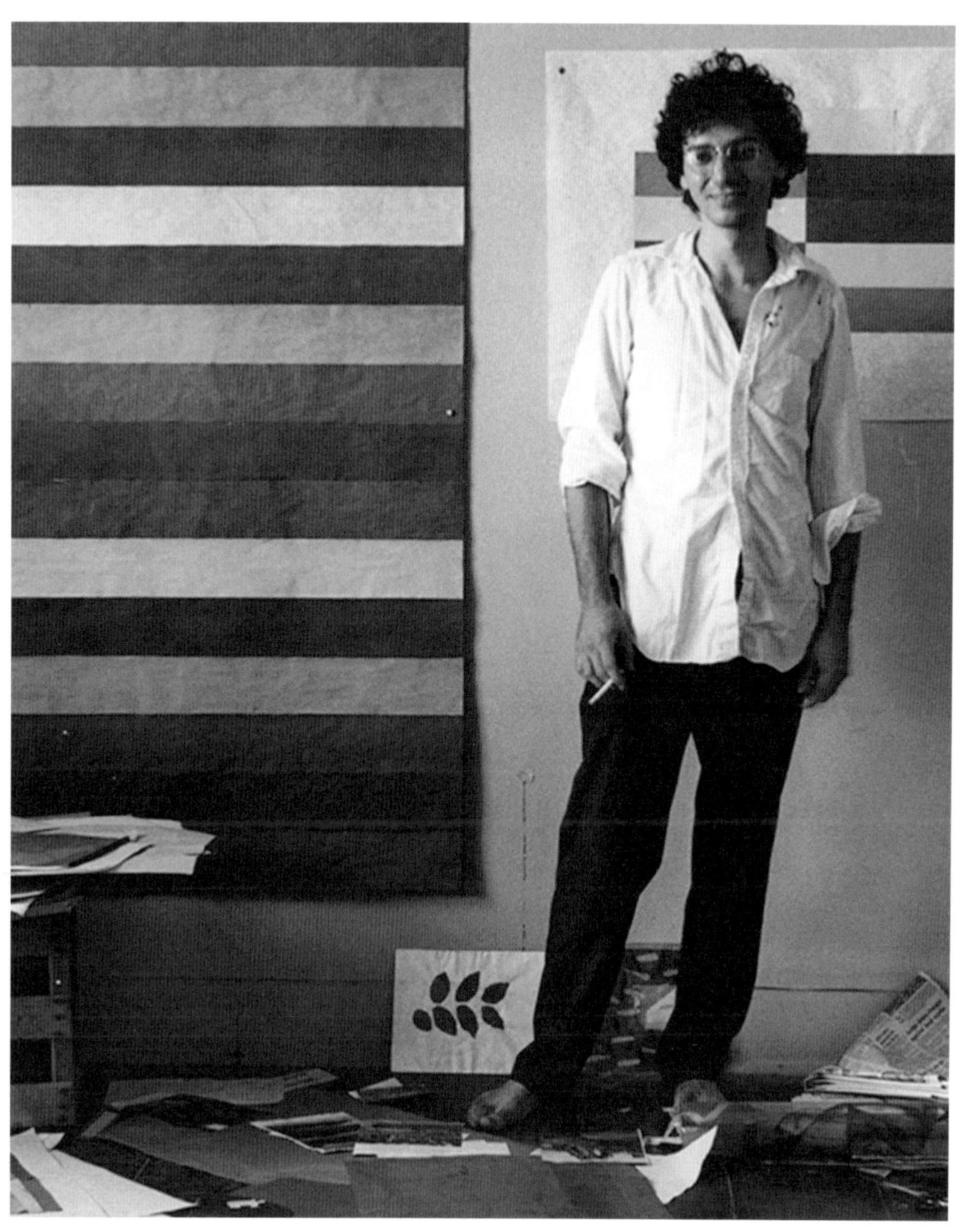

Richard Speer

Before the Fall: Peter Halley's Gouache Paintings 1977–78

Viewers familiar with Peter Halley's iconography since 1981—a rectilinear syntax of cells, prisons, and conduits diagramming isolation and technological metastasis in the postmodern metropolis—will find it revelatory to encounter the artist's paintings from the late 1970s, when he stood at the cusp of what was to become his definitive style. While in many ways his paintings from 1977 and 1978 presaged impending developments in his work, their conceptual agenda was significantly different from those that followed. The paintings, all gouache on paper, reflected a host of contemporaneous influences, as well as aspects of the city in which they were painted, New Orleans, Louisiana. In light of their overlap with, and divergence from, his post-1981 paintings, it is intriguing that on both sides of that pivotal divide, Halley adopted essentially the same strategy: deploying the vocabulary of geometric abstraction to articulate forms that are in fact pointedly referential.

The context of these works is interwoven with key art movements of the 1970s. Among these were New Image Painting, which sought a return to representation after Minimalism's unremitting formalism; and the Pattern and Decoration movement, which, along with Feminist Art, posited alternatives to the hegemony of entrenched patriarchal structures in art and culture. Peter Halley, erudite in the history of modernism and particularly immersed in the aesthetics of Henri Matisse, was also drawn to the art of Meso-America, Africa, and the Middle East. As an artist committed to the possibilities of the straight line, he was deeply curious about the application of rectilinear geometry within pictorial systems unbeholden to the Western canon. "The movements I was interested in," he reflects, "had rejected the model of Western European art and industrialized culture and were looking to non-Western, non-paternalistic sources as a foundation on which to form a cultural ethos." The gouaches were part of an inquiry into motifs that fascinated him in non-Western art. In them we find nods to Native American and Meso-American traditions: abstracted landscape/skyscapes that reference the step patterns of Navajo art, abstracted trees inspired by Hopi kachina figures, and depictions of the teepee dwellings of the Plains Indians. There are references to Islamic mosques, tombs, shrines, and boats that recall Egyptian funerary barques.

As this was also an era of new approaches to comparative religion and the emergence of multicultural studies, Halley made a point to intersperse Western images among the non-Western, including highly stylized depictions of the Christian cross and the crucifixion of Jesus. Art-historical references also abound: homages to Matisse's reclining figures and bathing nudes; the whimsically titled "Mondrian's Tree," which invokes the famously nature-averse neoplasticist by way of a twinkly, primary-colored grid straight out of "Broadway Boogie Woogie"; depictions of Persian tombs that slyly invert the compositional schema of Kenneth Noland; a visual pun at the expense of Renaissance chiaroscuro in the one of the "Crucifixion" paintings of 1978 (one of Christ's legs is black, the other white); and an acknowledgement of Pop Art's appropriation of unconventional and lowbrow media via craft-store stars and stickers in the "Boat" and "Teepee" paintings. (Halley's use of unconventional materials would continue in the 1980s and beyond with his appropriation of Roll-a-Tex, a texture additive for house paint, and a motley assortment of print media, among them vacuum-formed plastic and molded fiberglass.)

Across the breadth of their subject matter, the gouaches have a graphic economy and quasi-Jungian archetypalism very much in the vein of New Image Painting. In a reappraisal of the 1978 exhibition "New Image Painting" at the Whitney Museum of American Art, Roberta Smith, writing in 1987 in *The New York Times*, noted the movement's influence on Halley. "The taut, hard-edged silhouettes of [Joe] Zucker and [Robert] Moskowitz," she wrote, "have been connected with those of Philip Taaffe and Peter Halley... Halley's factory and electric battery shapes in particular suggest a kind of abstracted, geometric New Imagery." In my January 2017 interview with Halley, he confirmed the link: "I've never been able to see abstract art as abstract. And so the first time I saw one of Joel Shapiro's house sculptures or Jennifer Bartlett's huge piece, 'Rhapsody,' with geometric houses and landscapes, they totally made sense to me." His work from this period, he adds, "was about turning geometry into images, but unlike my present work, the images were drawn from ethnology and based on symbolic representations of the rhythms of nature as underlying truths about the world. They had symbolic resonance to me at the time."

The paintings are rooted not only in their time, but also in their sense of place. Born and raised in Manhattan, Halley had first come to New Orleans in the summer of 1973 and was invigorated by the city's sultry climate and dynamic cultural mélange. He stayed a year, then returned to the Northeast, graduating from Yale University in 1975 with an undergraduate degree in art history (his senior thesis was on Matisse). Afterwards he returned to New Orleans, which became his home base as he traveled in Central America and North Africa, studying pre-Columbian and Islamic art and architecture. He also entered the University of New Orleans's M.F.A. program, from which he graduated in 1978. Halley responded strongly to the "intensified sense of color" he experienced in Louisiana, and indeed, the gouache paintings fairly hum with highly pitched vibrational chromaticism. Although the region's glowing, humidity-diffused sunlight and flamboyantly painted buildings did not give the artist his predilection for vivid color—it was already established—they certainly affirmed and reinforced it.

To live in and ambulate through this atmosphere also played into Halley's youthful idylls of a Matissean Eden, with the Gulf of Mexico standing in for the Mediterranean. "What I remember so distinctly," he remarks of his first trip to New Orleans, "is going there in college with friends, driving straight through, taking turns at the wheel, and finally hitting the Gulf Coast—getting out of the car at a gas station and seeing the Gulf of Mexico for the first time—and thinking that here, finally, was this place similar to how one would feel about the Mediterranean: a kind of Middle Sea of semi-tropical conditions and the comforting, relaxing quality of the warm breeze." It is worth noting, vis-à-vis Matisse, that some of Halley's "Boat" paintings from 1977 are gouache collages, obliquely recalling Matisse's late-career gouache cut-outs.

Given these aquatic environs, it would be tempting to interpret the sparkly checkerboard grids in "Fez" and the "Tree" paintings of 1977 as evocations of sunlight glinting off waves in the Gulf or the Mississippi River, but something different is at play in these works. While the grids' colors may seem arbitrary, like the frenetic dancing of prismatic light on water, Halley has in fact plotted the chromatic distribution quite meticulously, embedding images within subtle interactions of pattern. "Four Crosses" (1977) gives an initial impression of randomized color à la Ellsworth Kelly's "Spectrum Colors Arranged by Chance" (1951–53), but there is in fact an easy-to-miss repeating pattern subsumed within its grid of shimmering squares. "What many artists were doing at the time," he says, "was taking strategies from Minimalist repetition, such as Kelly's colored grids, and turning it into something more dynamic."

It is worth noting that aspects of the gouaches' imagery presage Halley's subsequent compositions. A "Tree" painting from 1977—red square atop white platform, blue rectangle branching down beneath it—seems prototypical of the cell-and-underground conduit compositions he took up in the early 80s. A 1977 painting of the Kaaba in Mecca, the most sacred site of Islam, predates by 36 years his series of paintings referencing the Kaaba, which debuted in a 2013 exhibition at Mottahedan Projects in Dubai. A 1977 piece depicting blocks of bold color, entitled "The Islamic Problem," looks ahead to a series of citrus-hued mixed grids he began exhibiting in early 2015. In his "Cross" studies and paintings of 1978, there is a muscular sense of permutation, of similar or identical compositions taken through varied color schemes for an Albers-like panoply of effects; this is a tactic Halley employs to this day. Finally, his modus operandi of distilling an image—teepee, boat, figure, tree—into a motif elegant enough to serve as a signifier, is the very strategy he applied in 1981 when he arrived at the iconic cells, prisons, and conduits that became the cornerstones of his mature pictorial lexicon.

Halley left New Orleans and returned to New York in 1980. He was 26 years old. Back in the vertical metropolis, with its dingy tenements and cold winters, he began making paintings that were very different from his New Orleans work. Despite its population density, New York can be a lonely city; Halley's feelings of isolation during this period dovetailed with his readings of Michel Foucault and Jean Baudrillard, whose respective emphases on the geometry of control and the transmogrification of subject into simulacrum had a seismic impact on his thinking. In 1981 he painted "The Prison of History," a menacing cinderblock façade with barred windows, and with that epiphanic piece, the erstwhile essentialism of his late-1970s work and mindset gave inexorably way to a career-long exploration of the often sinister forces mediating late-20th and early-21st century technology and society. As he would reflect in his 1990 essay, "Geometry and the Social," "the idea of a connection between geometry and the natural order—the idea that behind appearance there might be some kind of abstract order in nature...became impossible for me. I think at that time there was a watershed, reflected in many artists' work, after which many of the truisms about cross-cultural experience, nature, as well as various other claims associated with Modernism and modernity, became problematic."

It has now been nearly forty years since that sea-change in Halley's thought. To look back upon the late-70s gouaches from this remove is to re-encounter a worldview that feels, in a sense, prelapsarian. We infer imminent transitions: New Orleans to New York; New Image to Neo-Geo; idealism and romanticism to skepticism and post-structuralism; relative obscurity to the satisfactions and pressures of art-world renown; and a larger cultural trajectory from the earnestness of the Carter presidency and the exhilaration of the Sexual Revolution to the dual specters of the Reagan presidency and the AIDS epidemic. For Halley, as for the nation, these transitions were jarring and epochal. The gouache paintings, with their cheery checkerboards and gold-star appliqué, gaze at us across the divide as from another world. Is it possible for squares, rectangles, and the occasional triangle to engender nostalgia? If so, then the gouaches conjure up the sweet, heavy scents of the Vieux Carré: magnolia, bougainvillea, oleander, and the faintest whiff of apple blossom wafting through the garden.

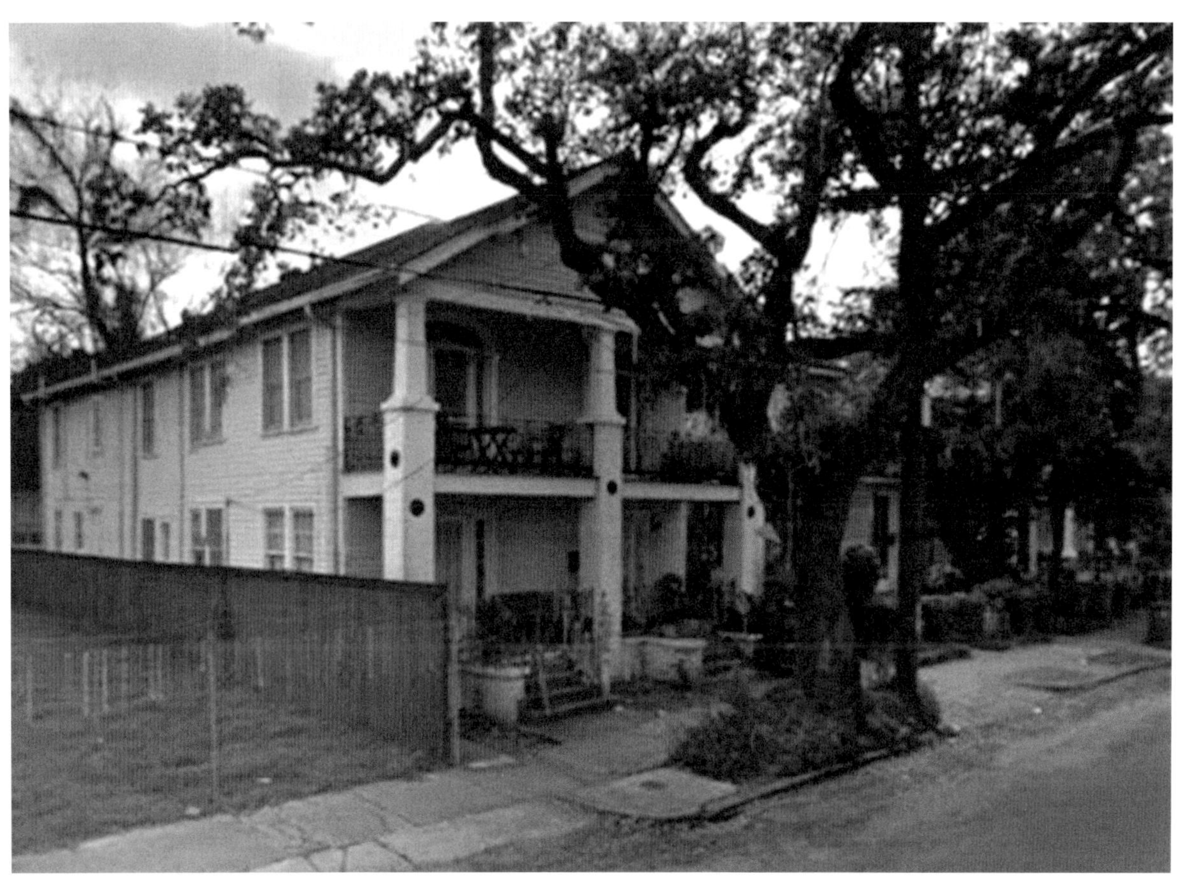

Boats

Boat, 1977, gouache on cut paper, 15 × 30 inches

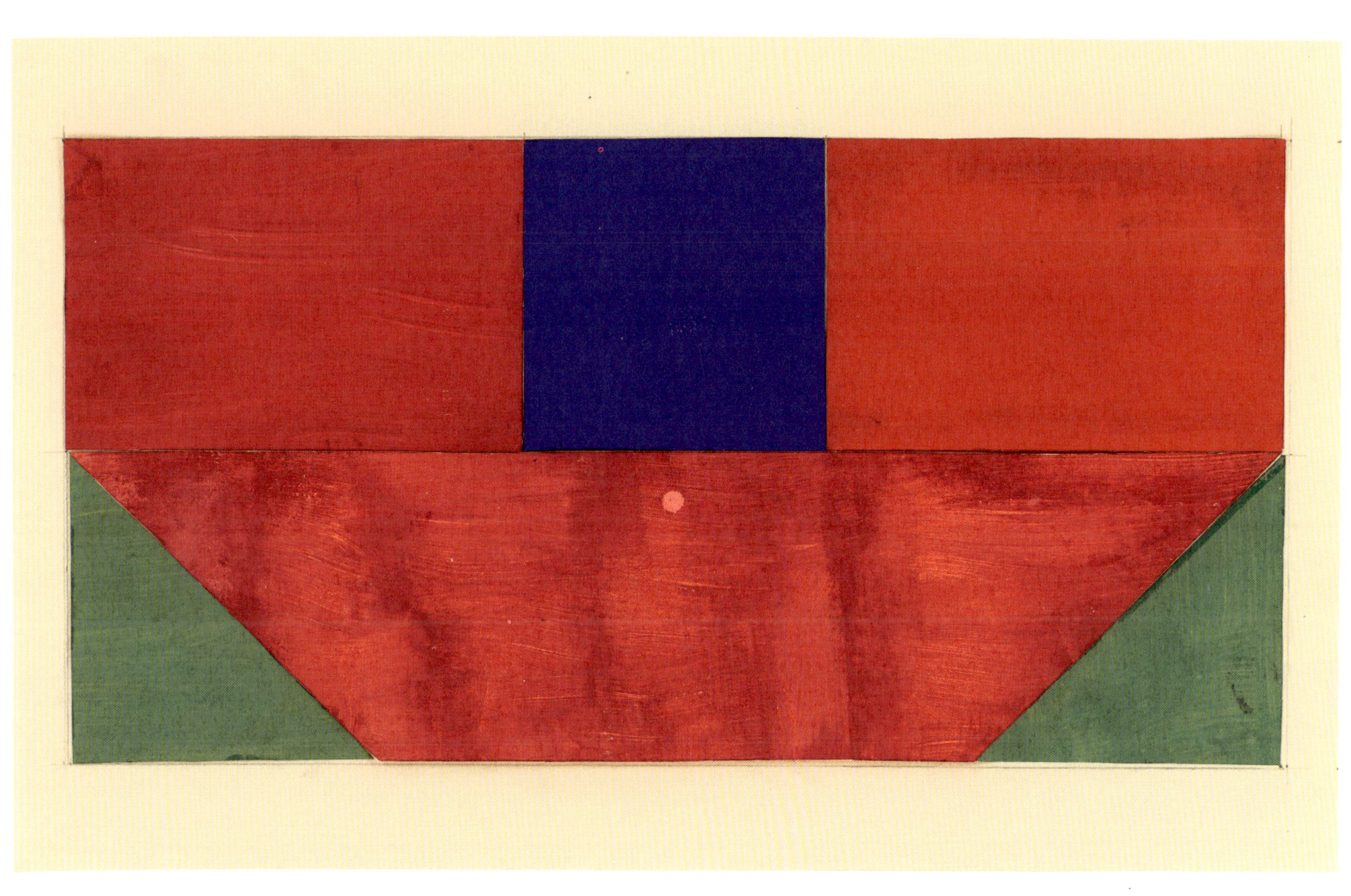

18 *Boat*, 1977, gouache on cut paper, 15 × 30 inches

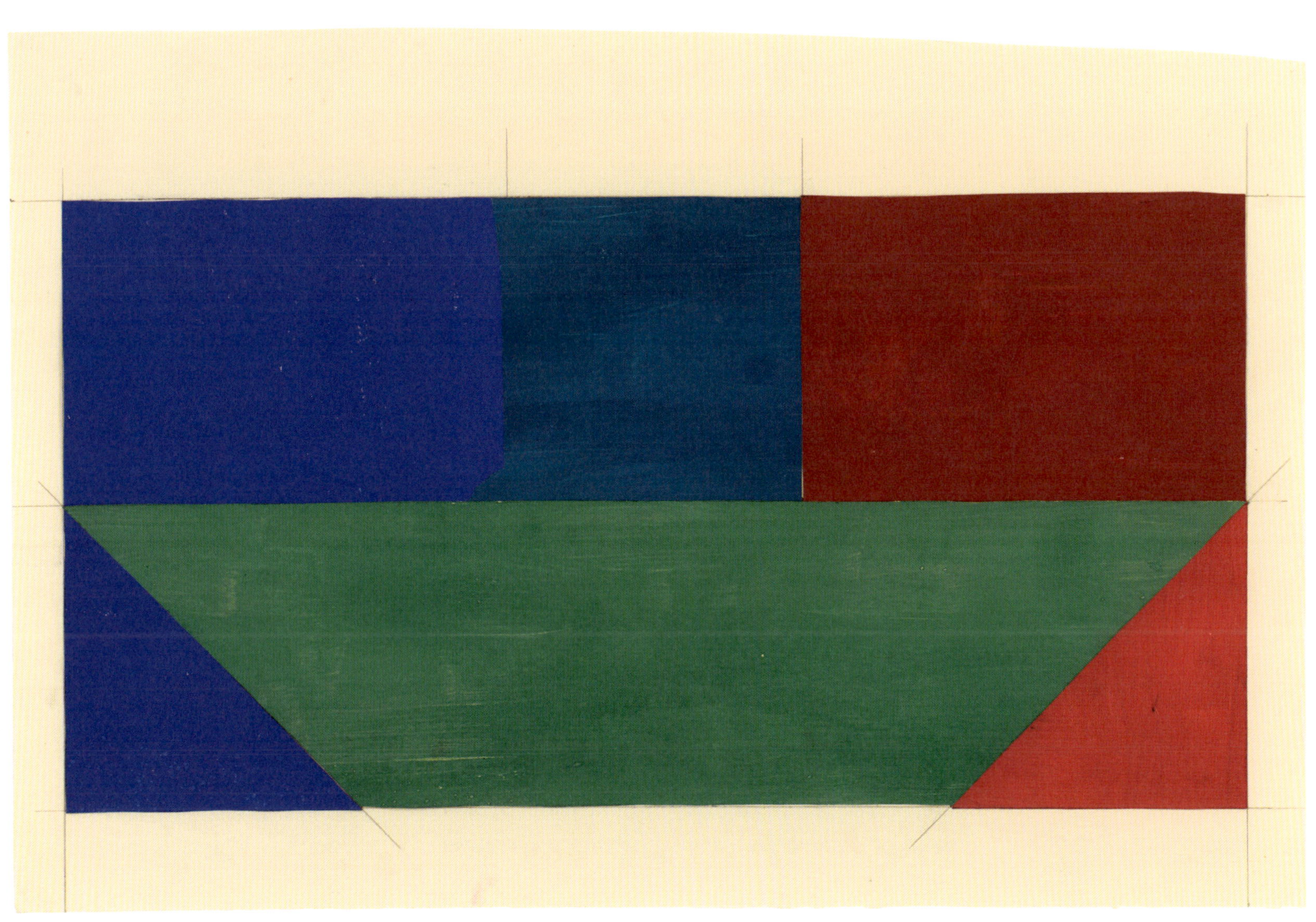

Boat, 1977, gouache, children's stickers and pencil on paper, 22 × 29½ inches

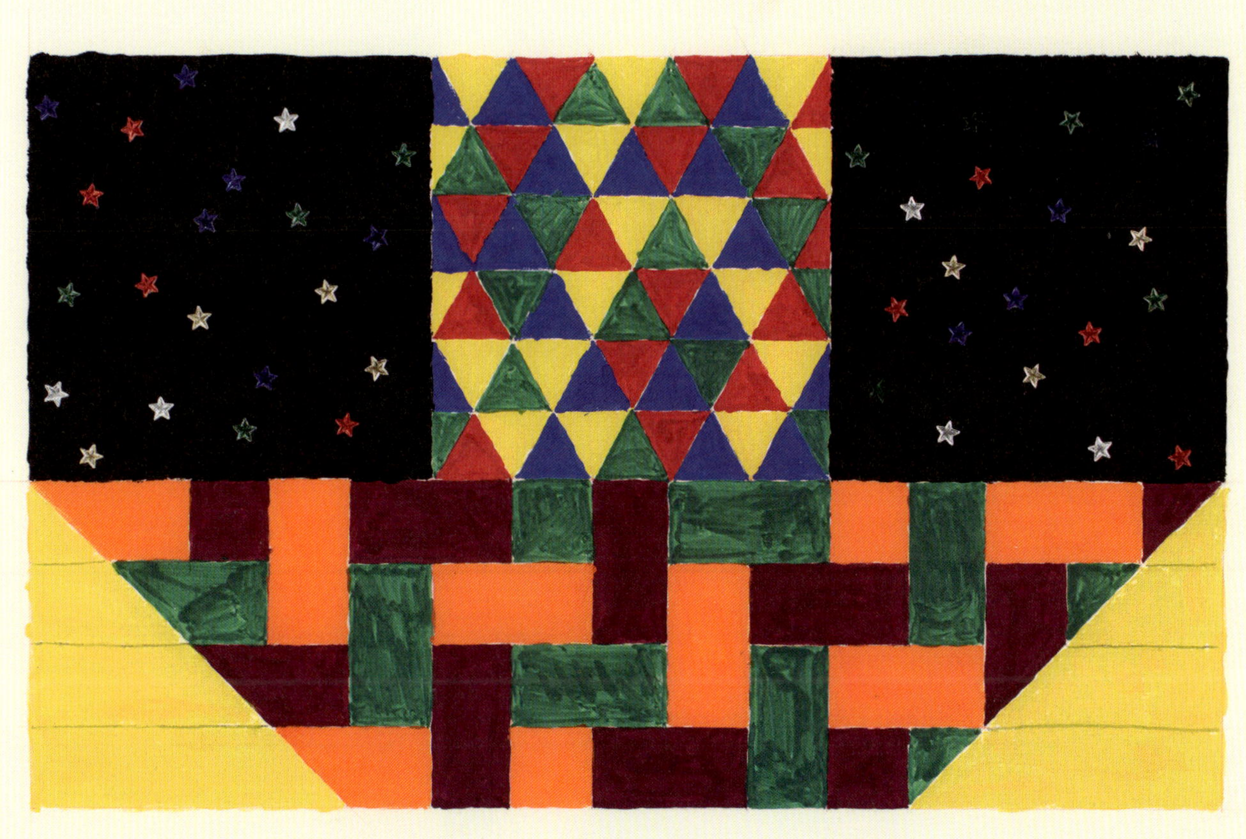

Boat, 1977, gouache, children's stickers and pencil on paper, 22 × 29½ inches

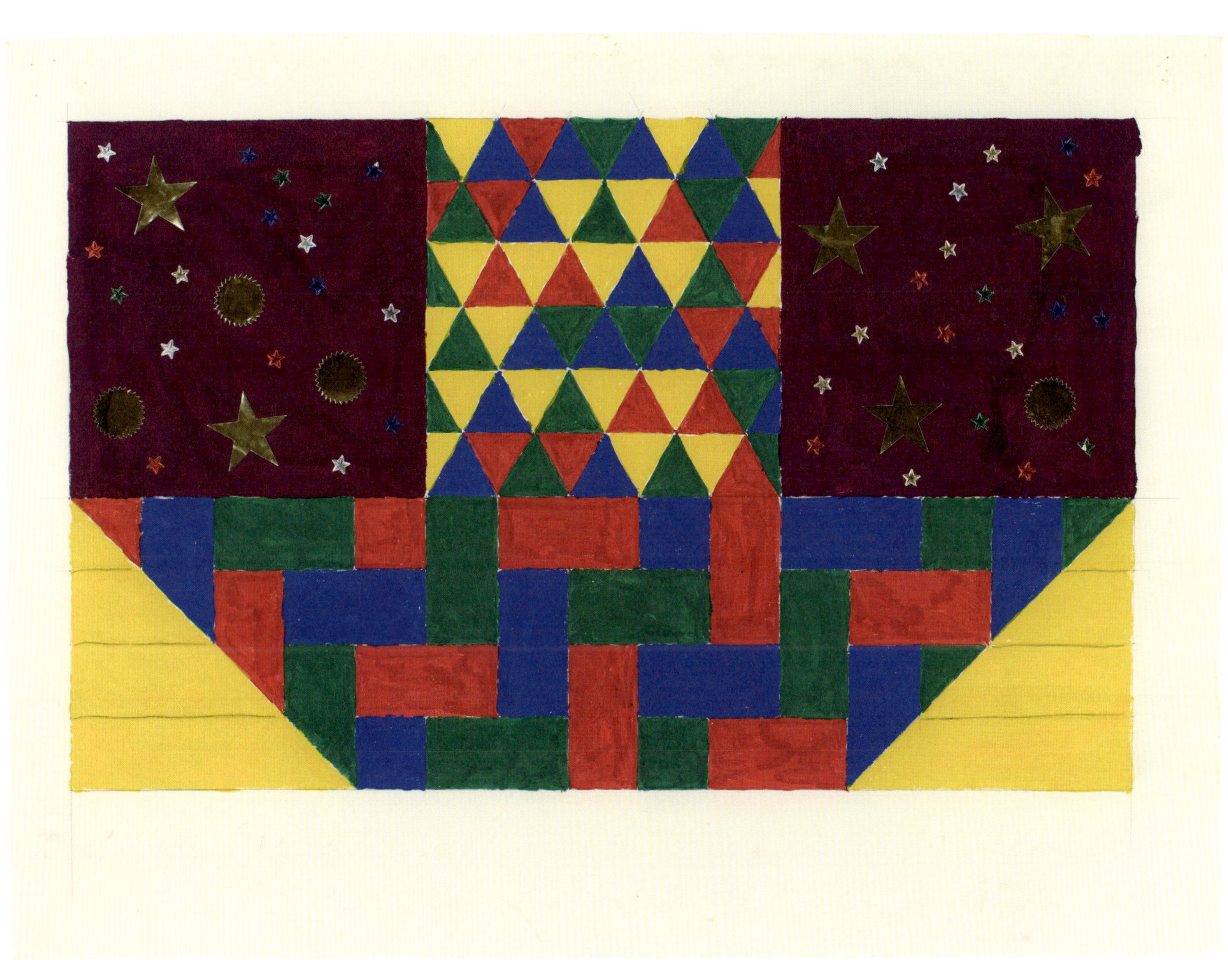

Boat, 1977, gouache, children's stickers and pencil on paper, 22 × 29½ inches

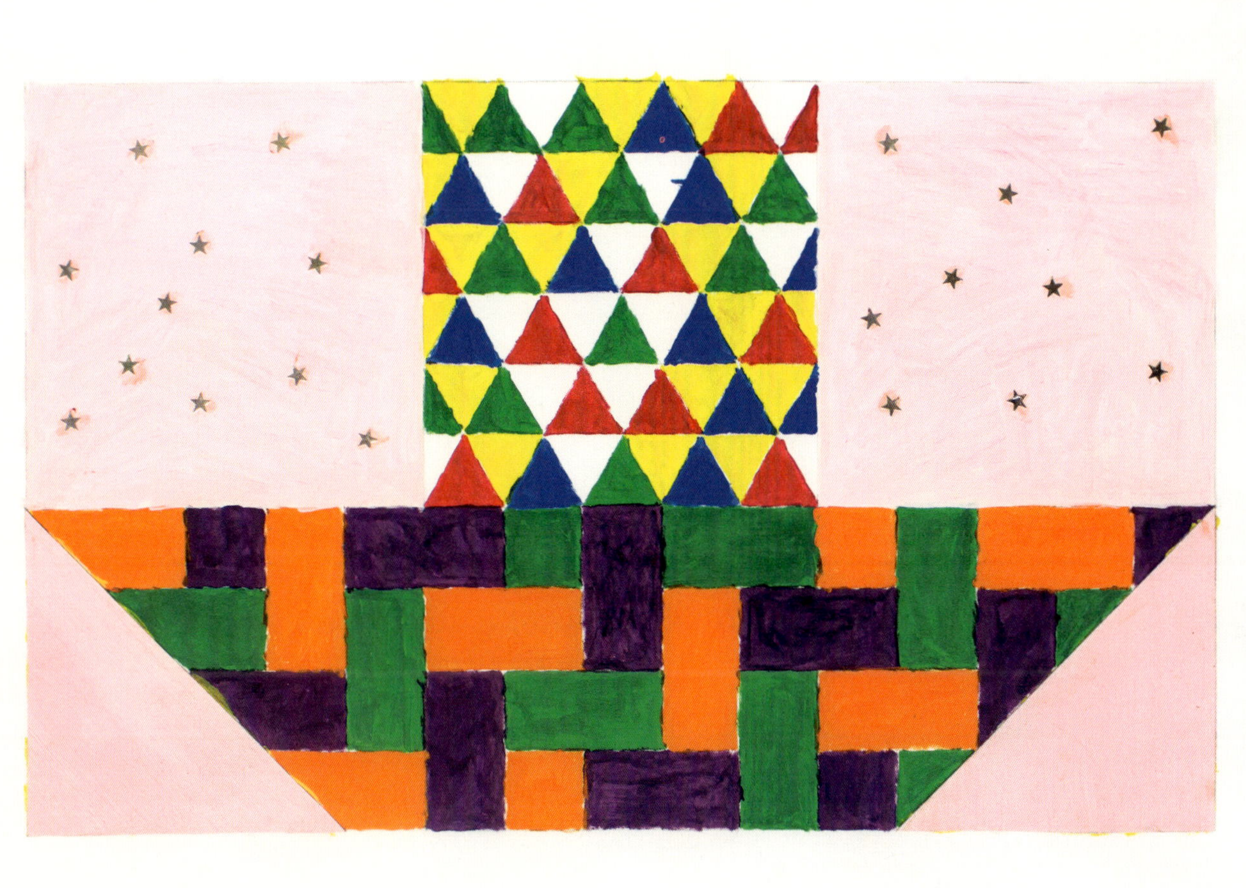

Stars

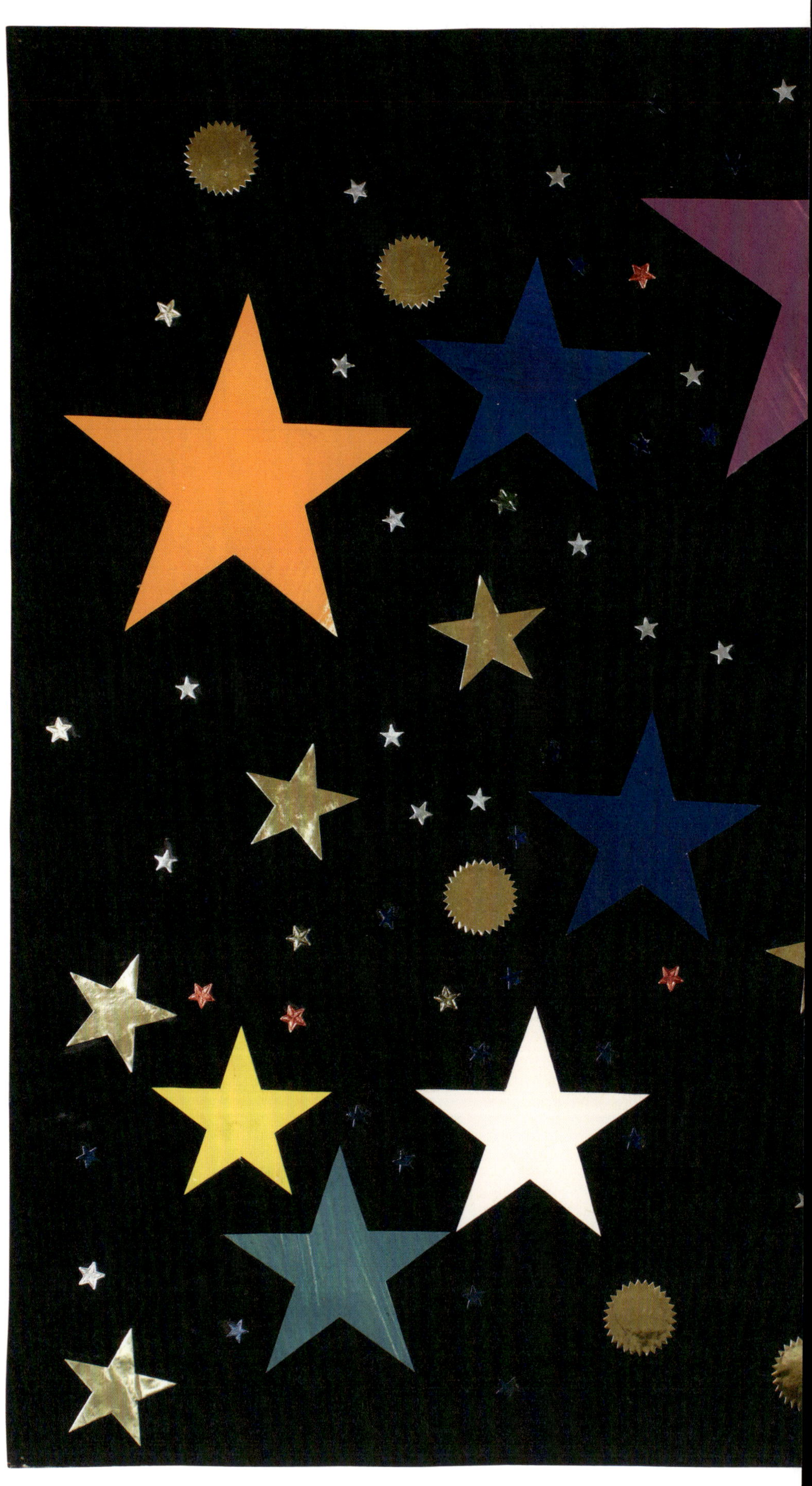

 Starry Night, 1977, gouache on paper collage, children's stickers on paper, 24¼ × 38½ inches

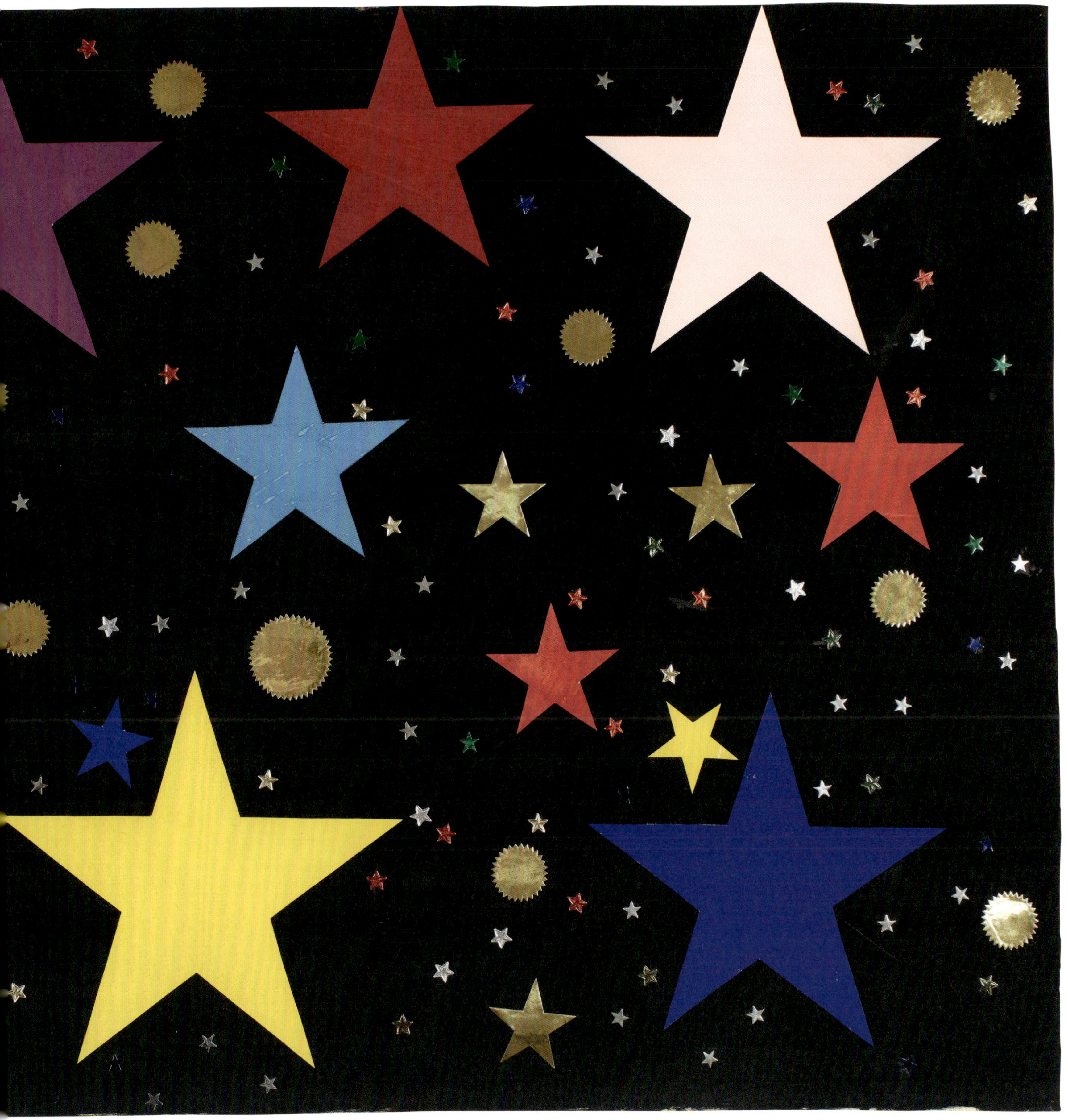

Teepees

 Teepee, 1978, gouache and pencil on paper, 16½ × 16½ inches

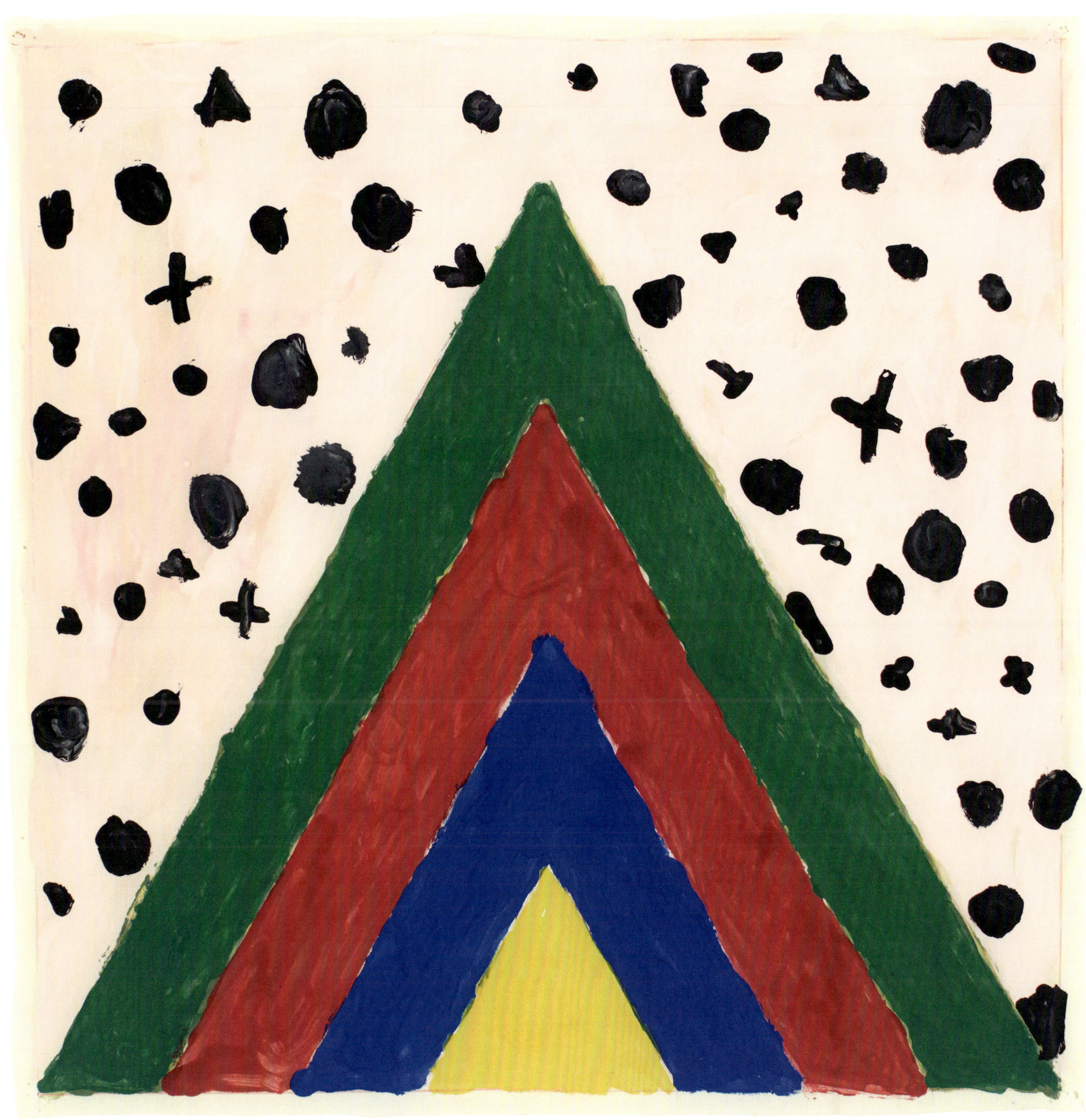

Teepee, 1978, gouache, children's stickers and pencil on paper, 16½ × 16½ inches

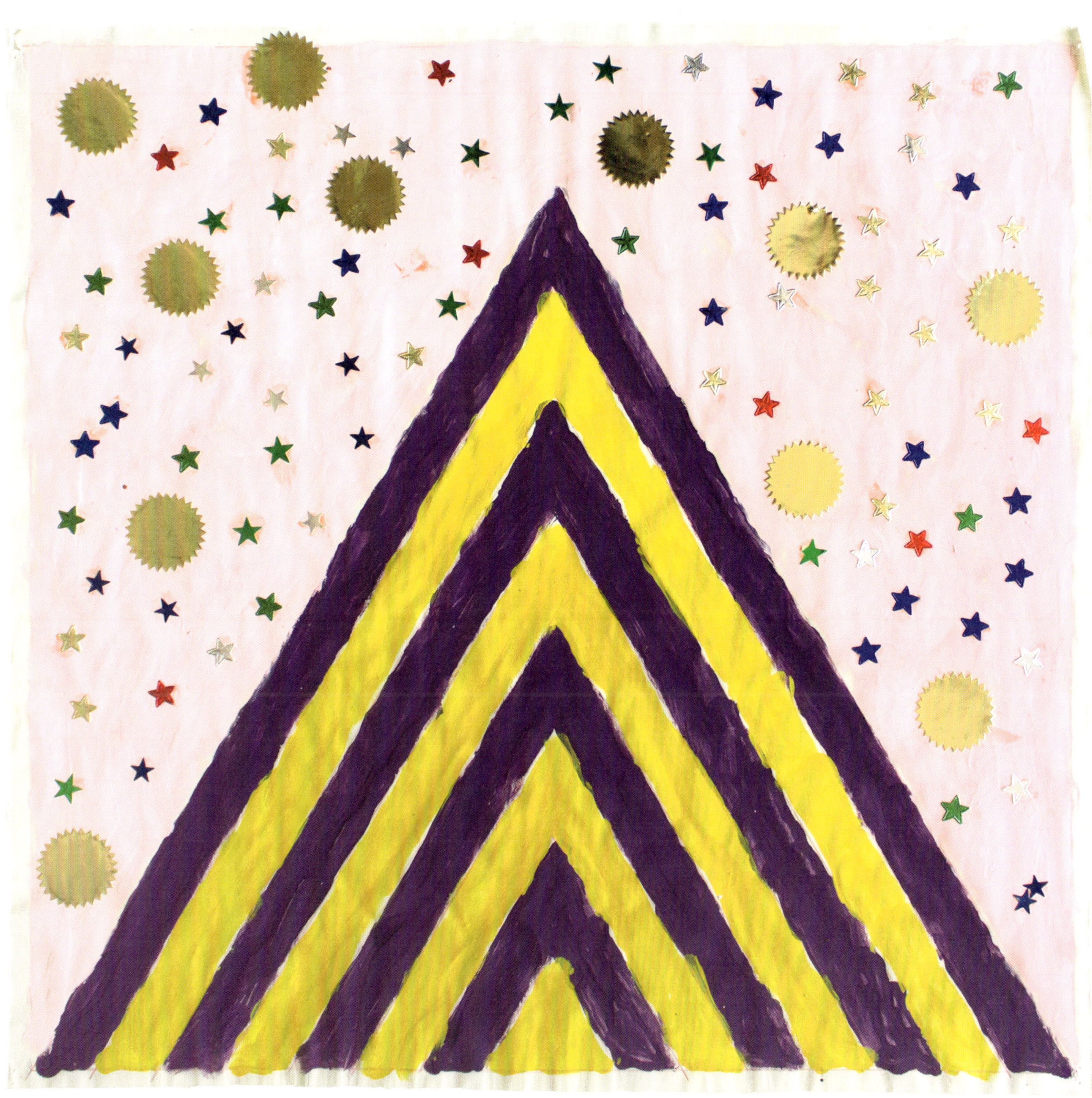

Landscapes with Sky

Landscape with Sky, 1977, gouache and pencil on paper, 15 × 15 inches

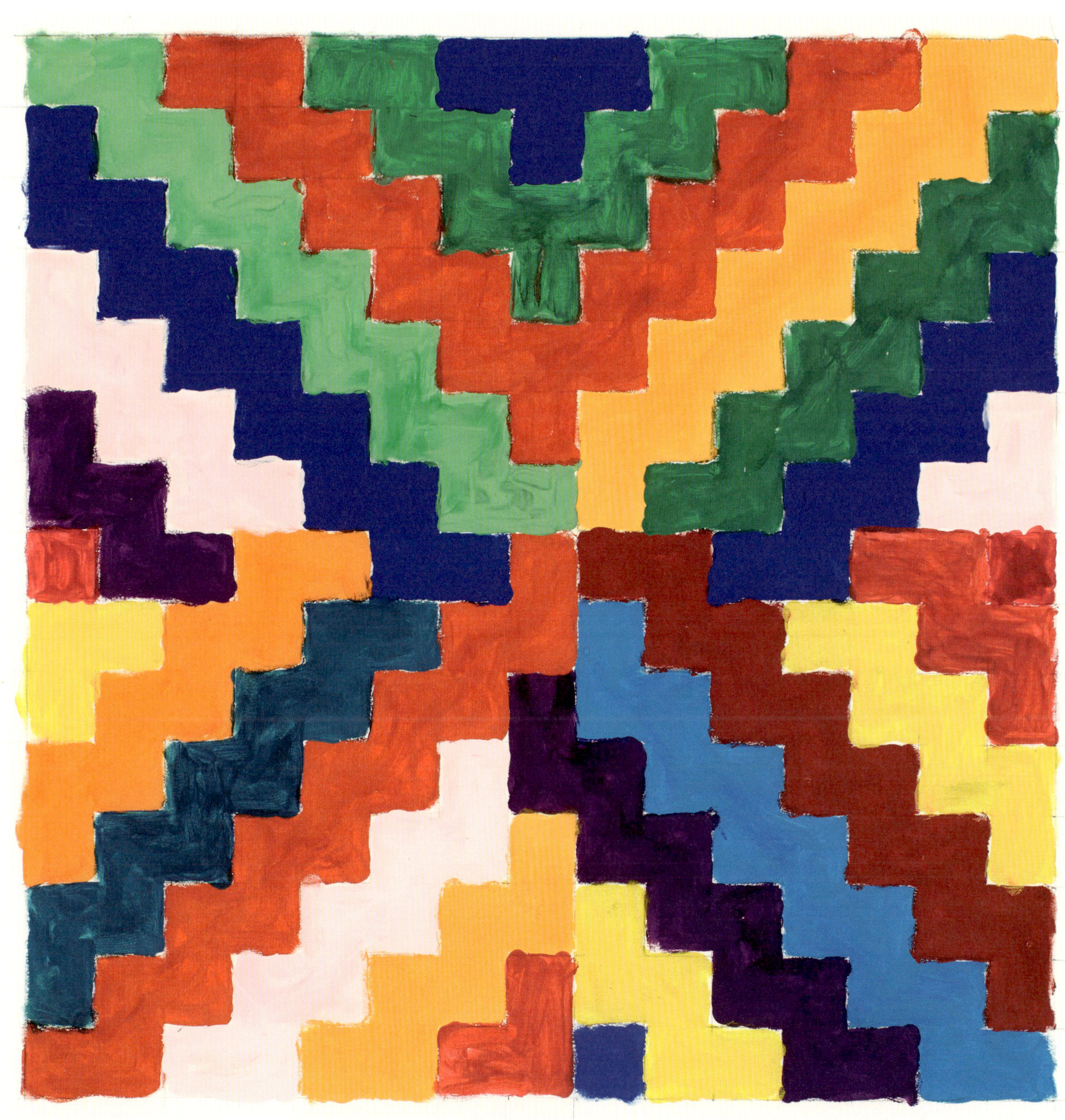

Landscape with Sky, 1977, gouache and pencil on paper, 14 × 14 inches

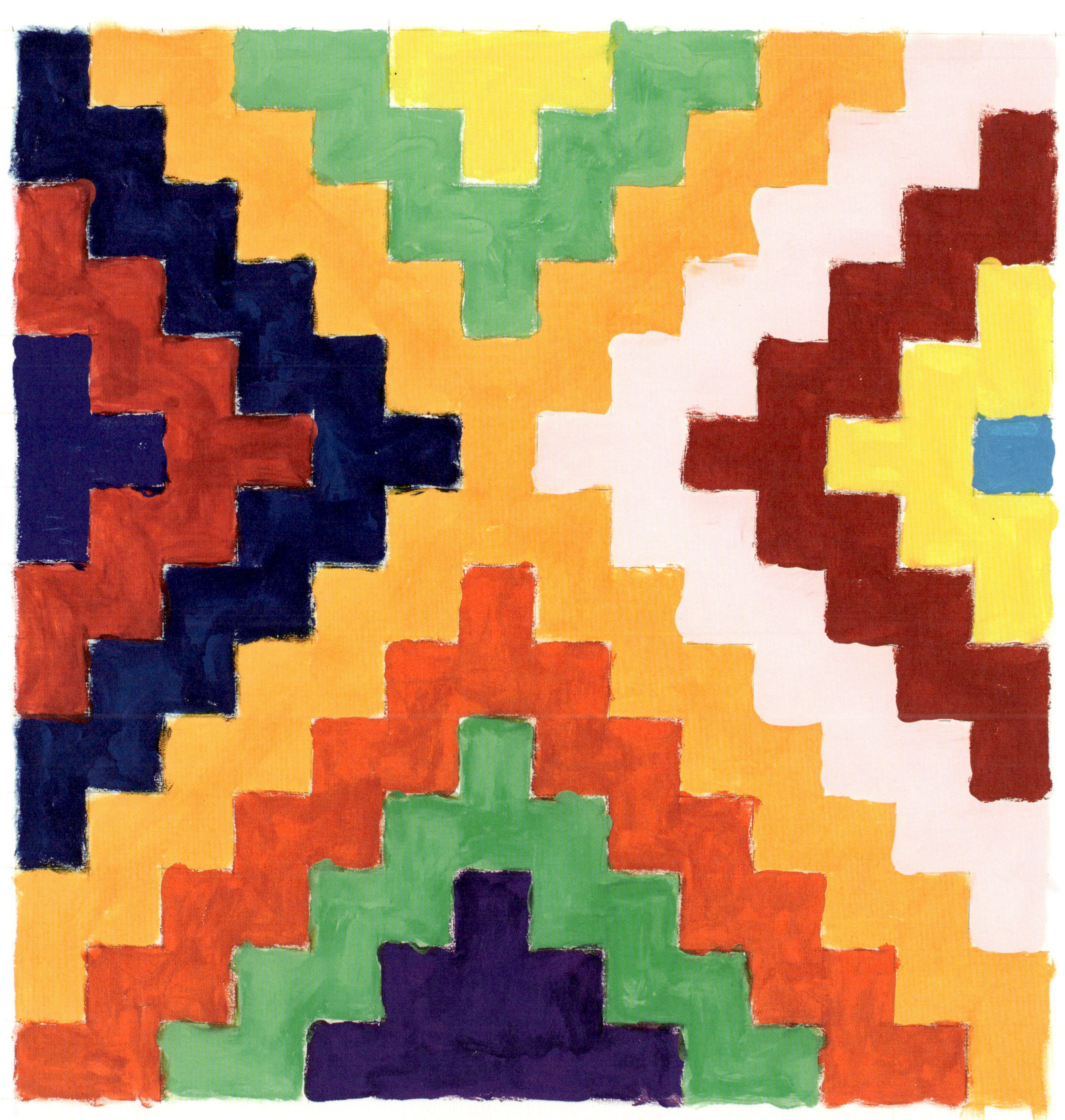

 Landscape with Sky, 1977, gouache and pencil on paper, 11 × 13 inches

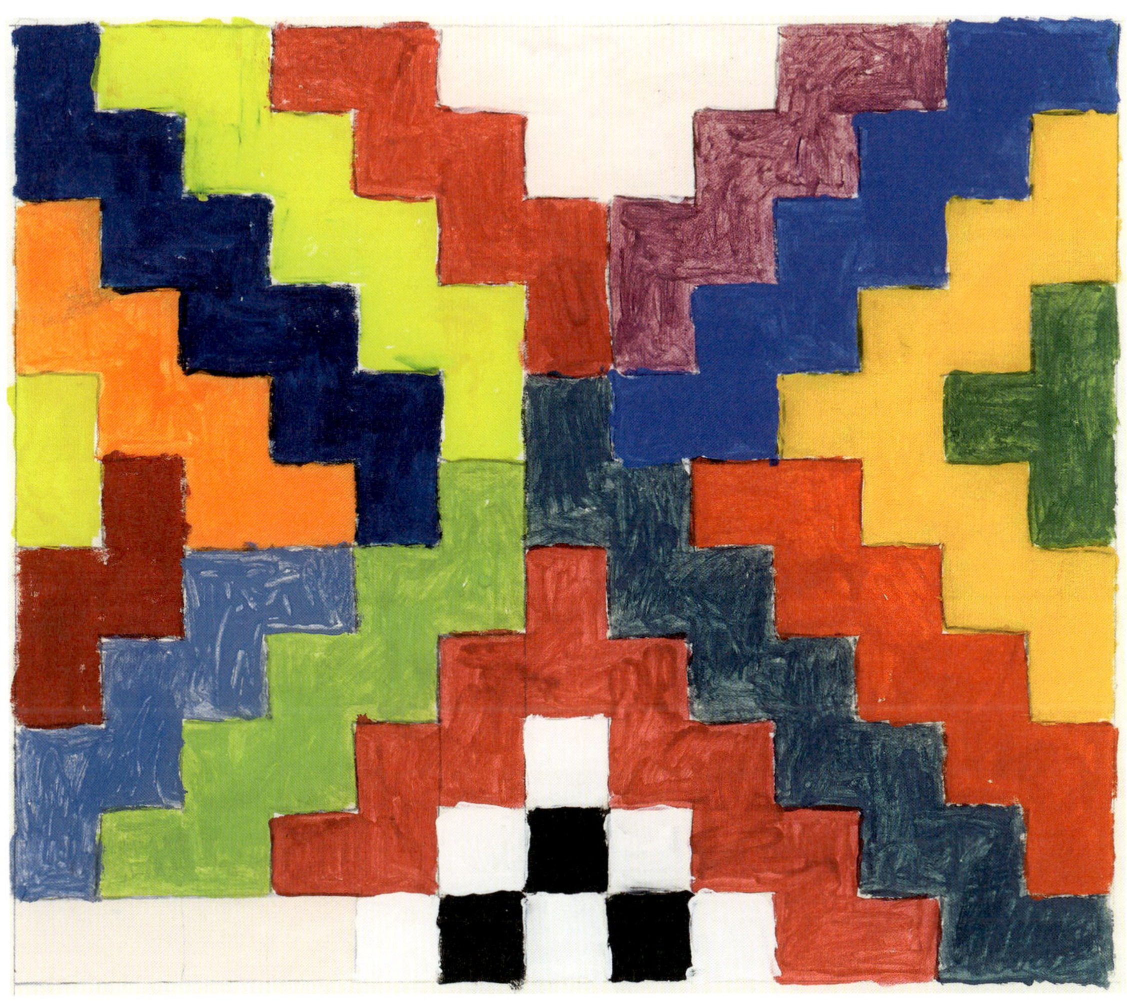

Landscape with Sky, 1977, gouache and pencil on paper, 9 × 9 inches

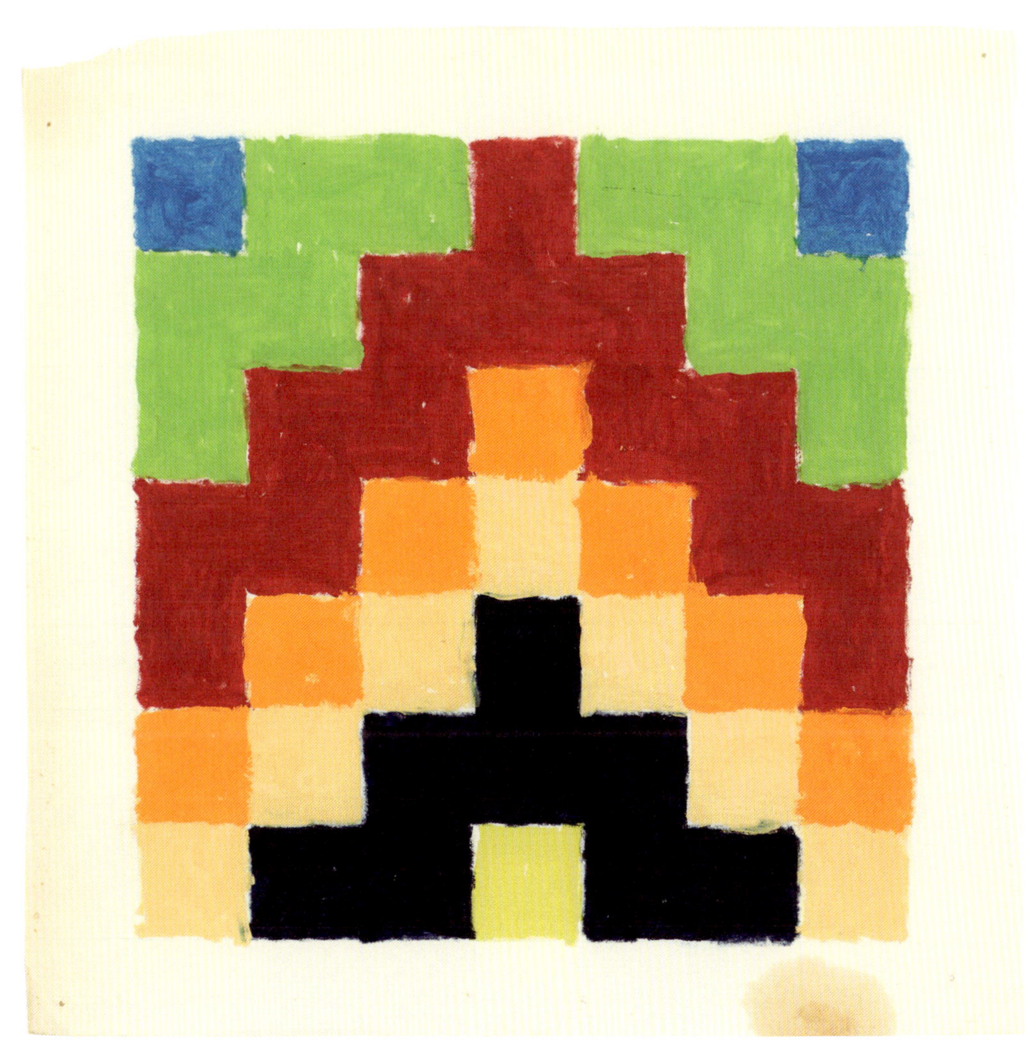

Islamic Influences

Kaaba, 1977, gouache and pencil on paper, 14 × 14 inches

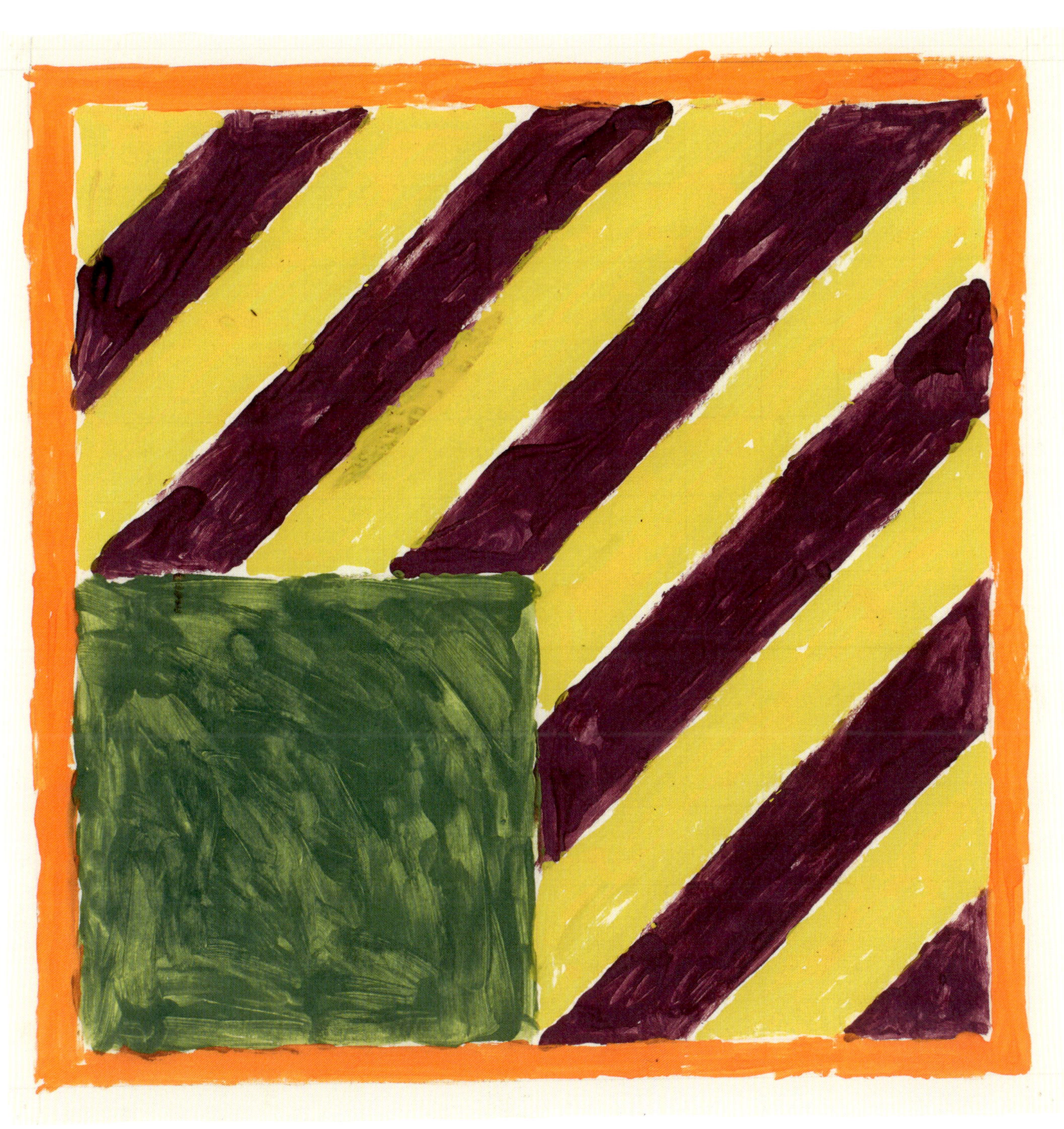

Fez, 1977, gouache and pencil on paper, 16 × 16 inches

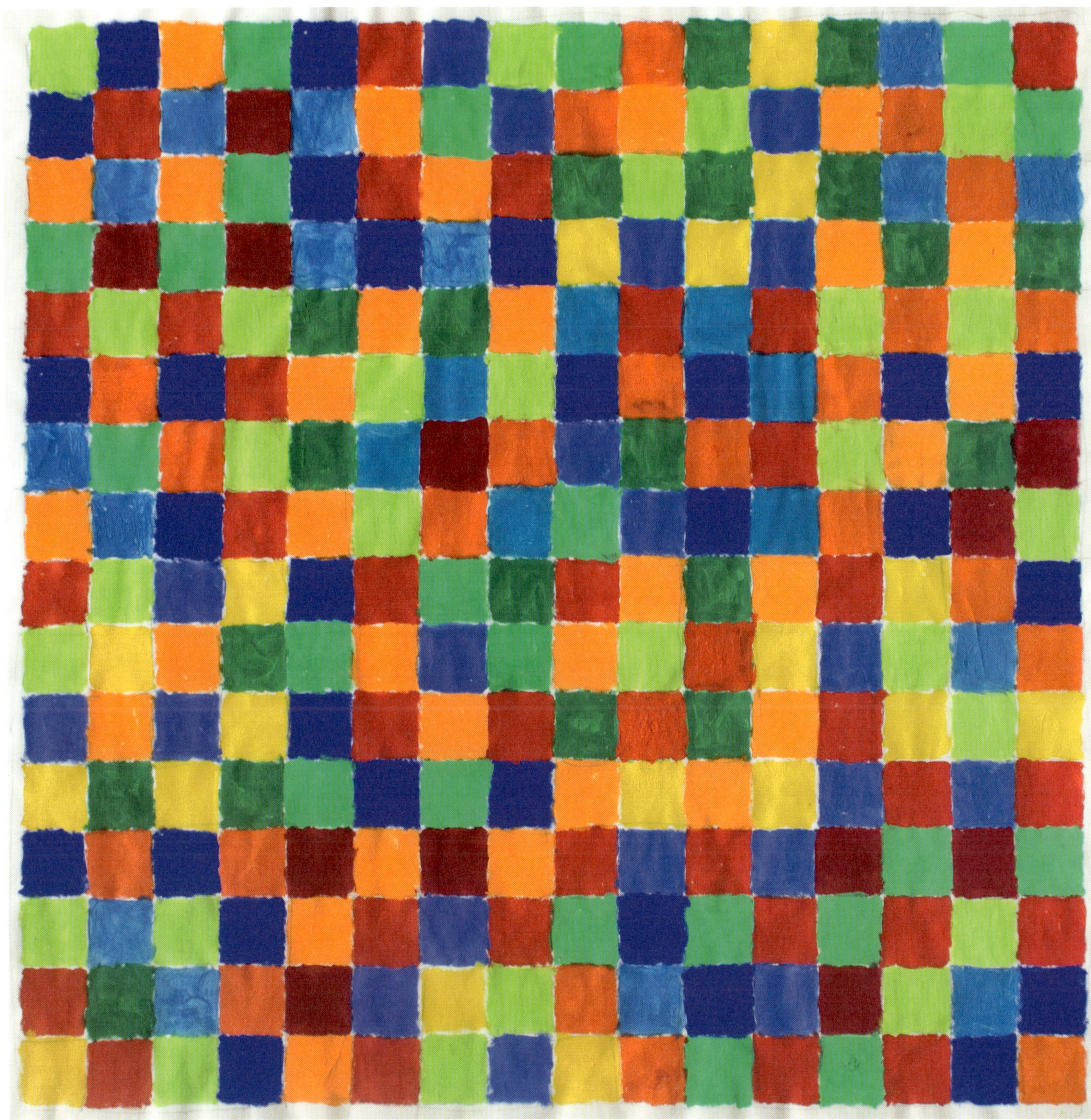

52 *Persian Tomb*, 1977, gouache, children's stickers, and pencil on paper, 19½ × 13 inches

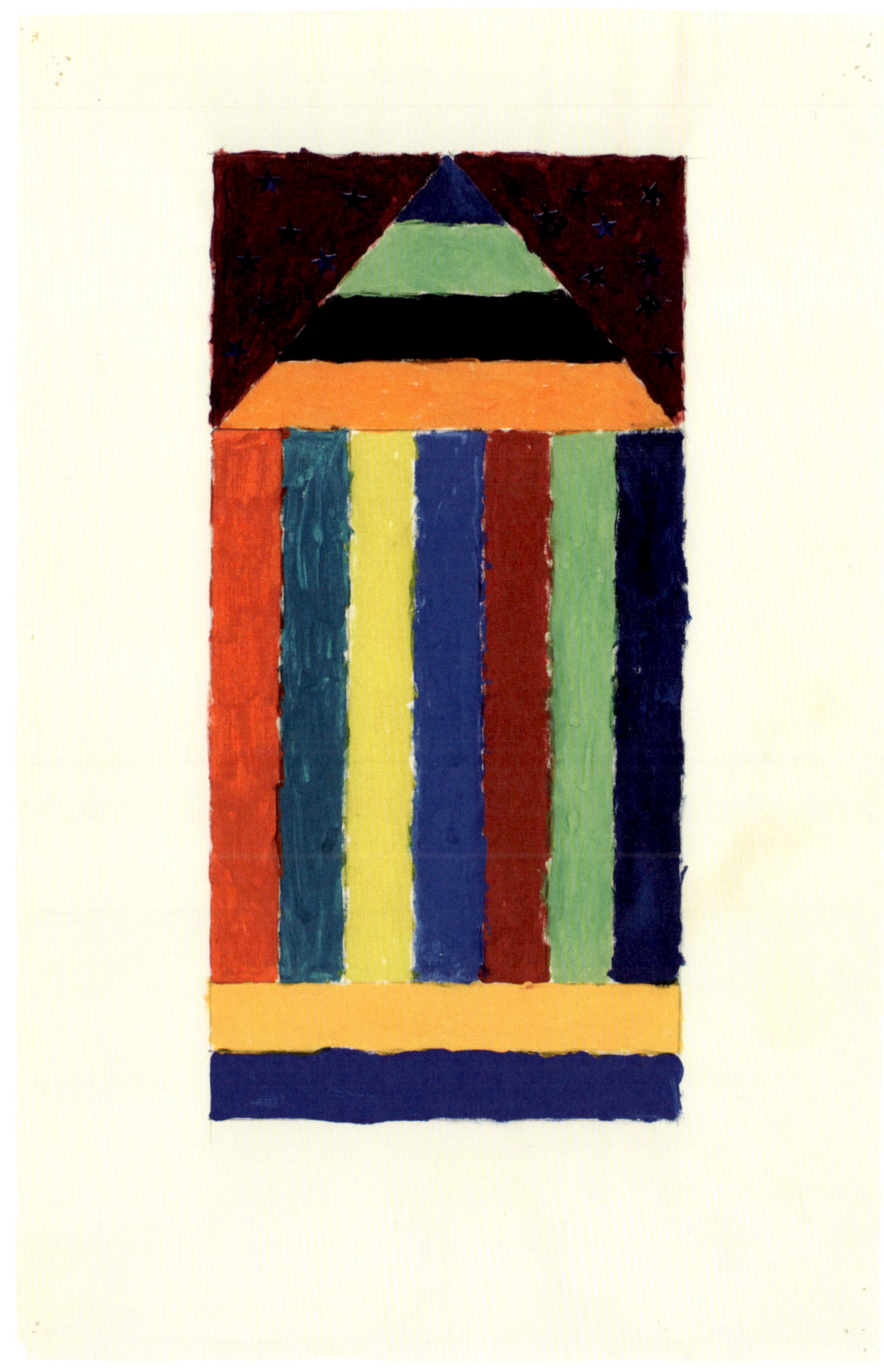

 Persian Tombs, 1977, gouache and pencil on paper, 22½ × 28 inches

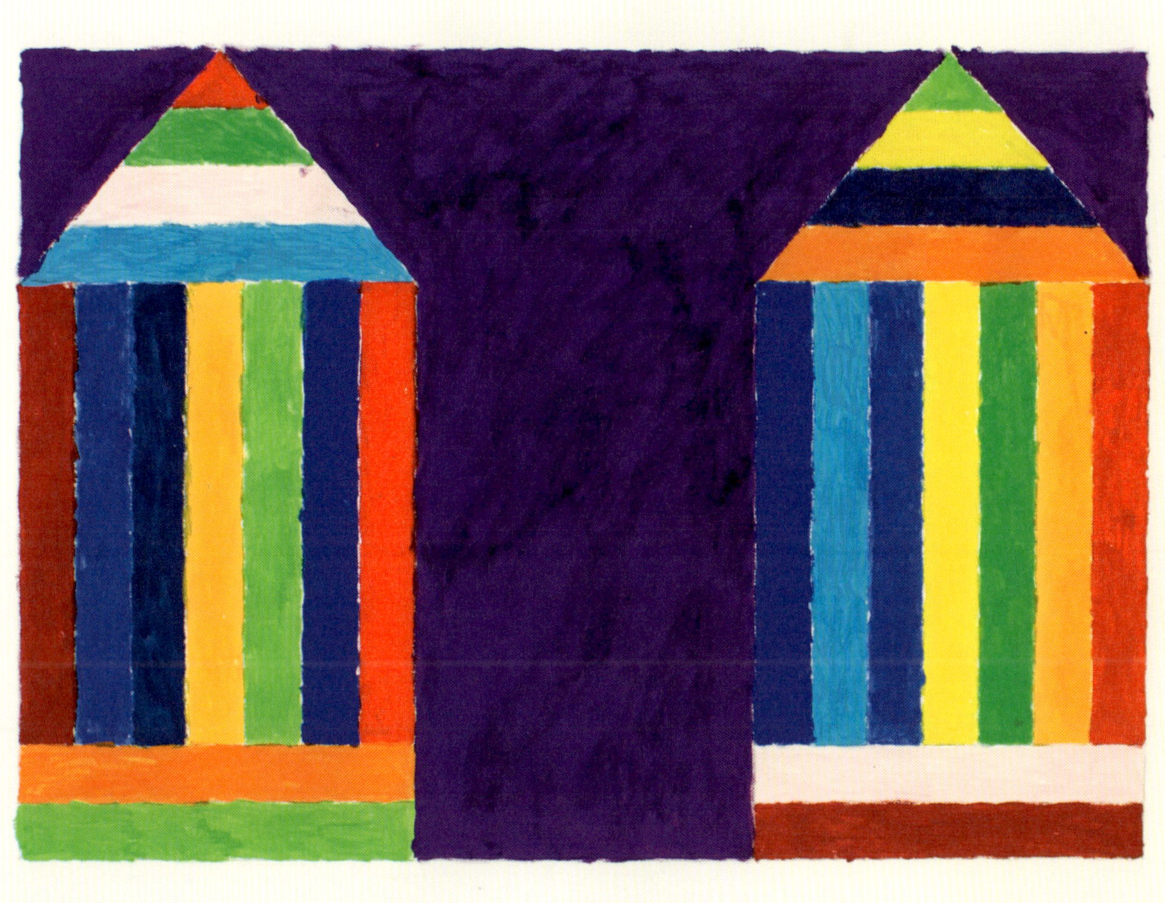

The Islamic Problem, 1977, gouache and pencil on paper, 28 × 22½ inches

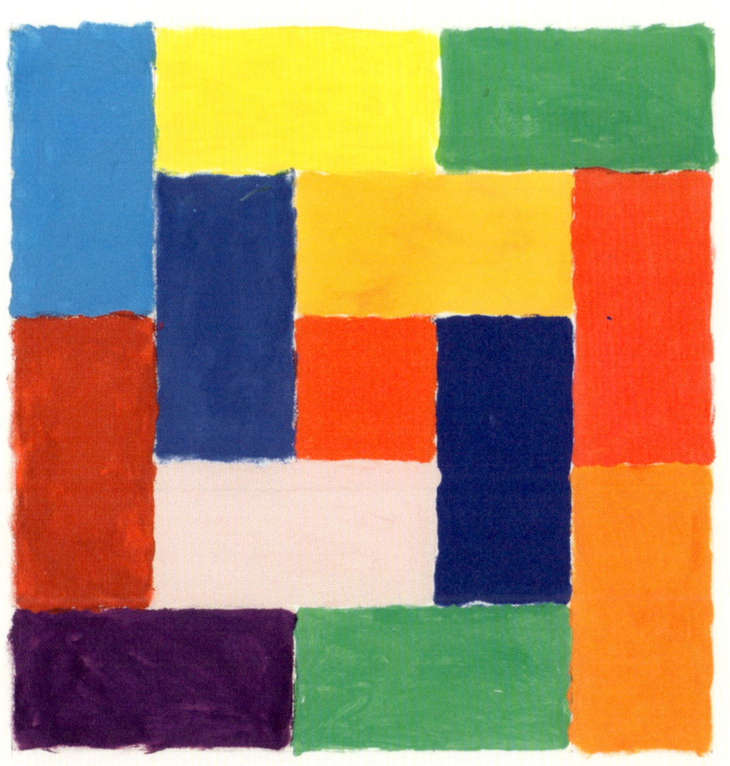
The Islamic Problem

 Two Trees, 1977, gouache on paper, 22½ × 28 inches

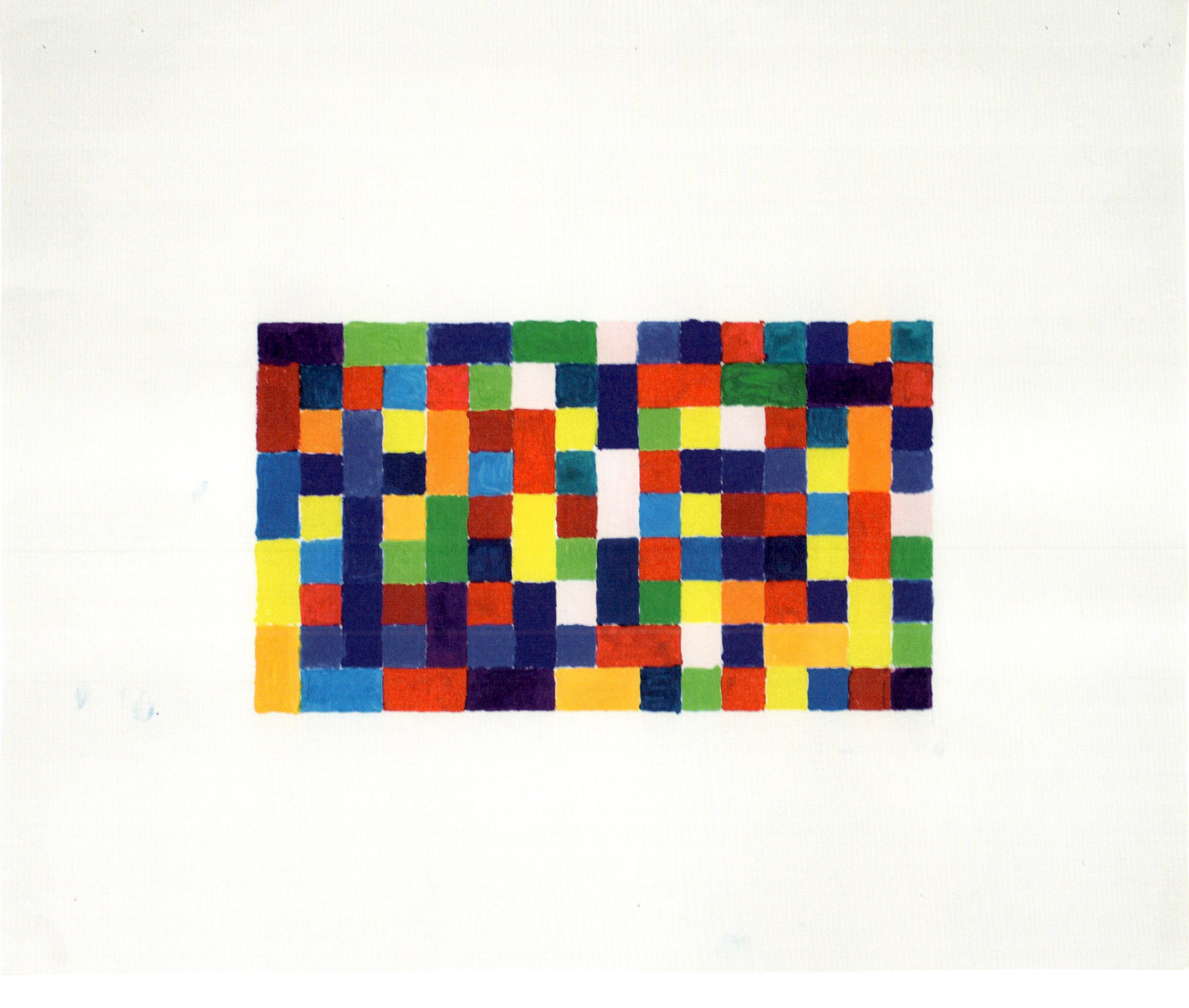

Mosque, 1978, gouache on paper, 8 × 9 inches

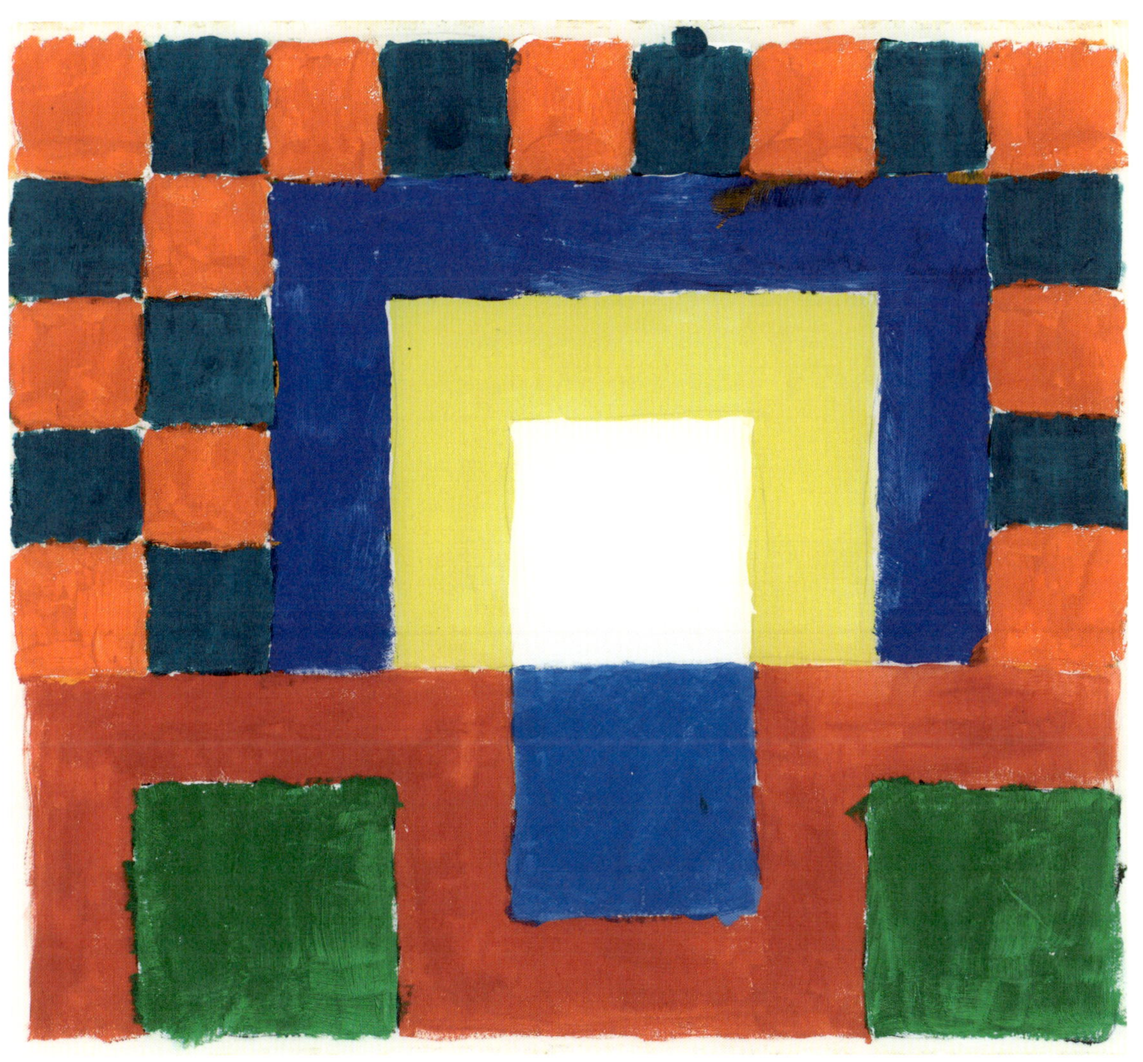

Crosses

64 *Two Crosses*, 1977, gouache on paper, 12 × 12 inches

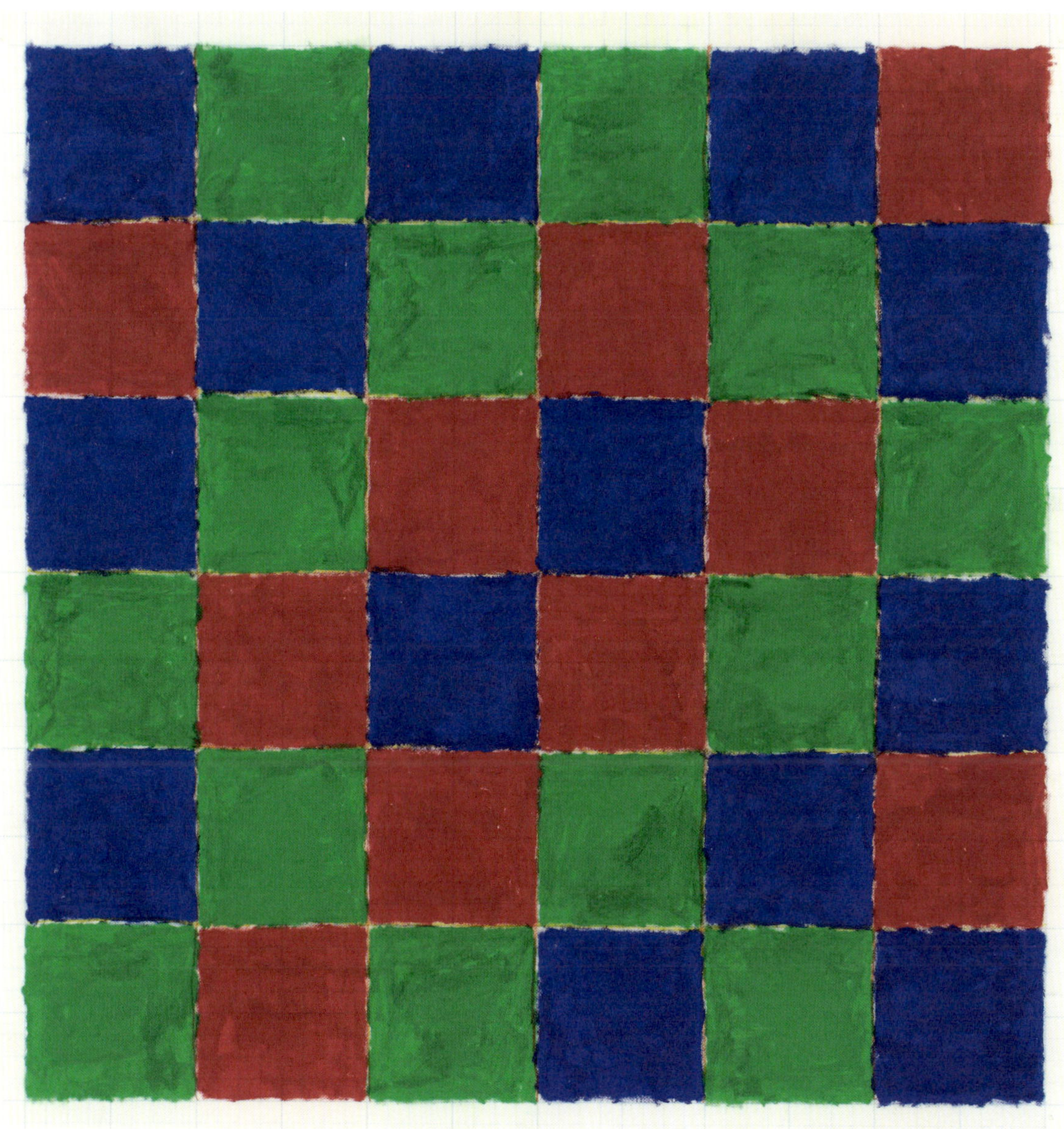

 Cross, 1977, gouache and pencil on paper with collage element, 8 × 8 inches

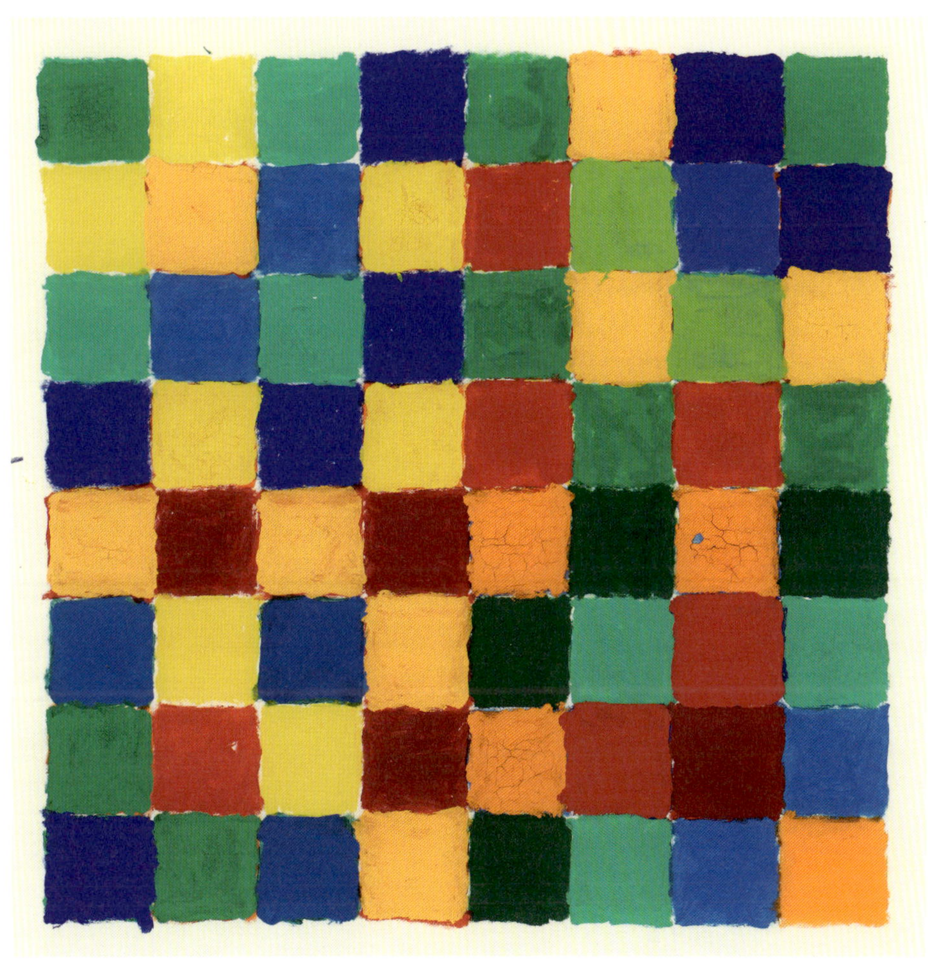

Four Crosses, 1977, gouache on paper, 12 × 12 inches

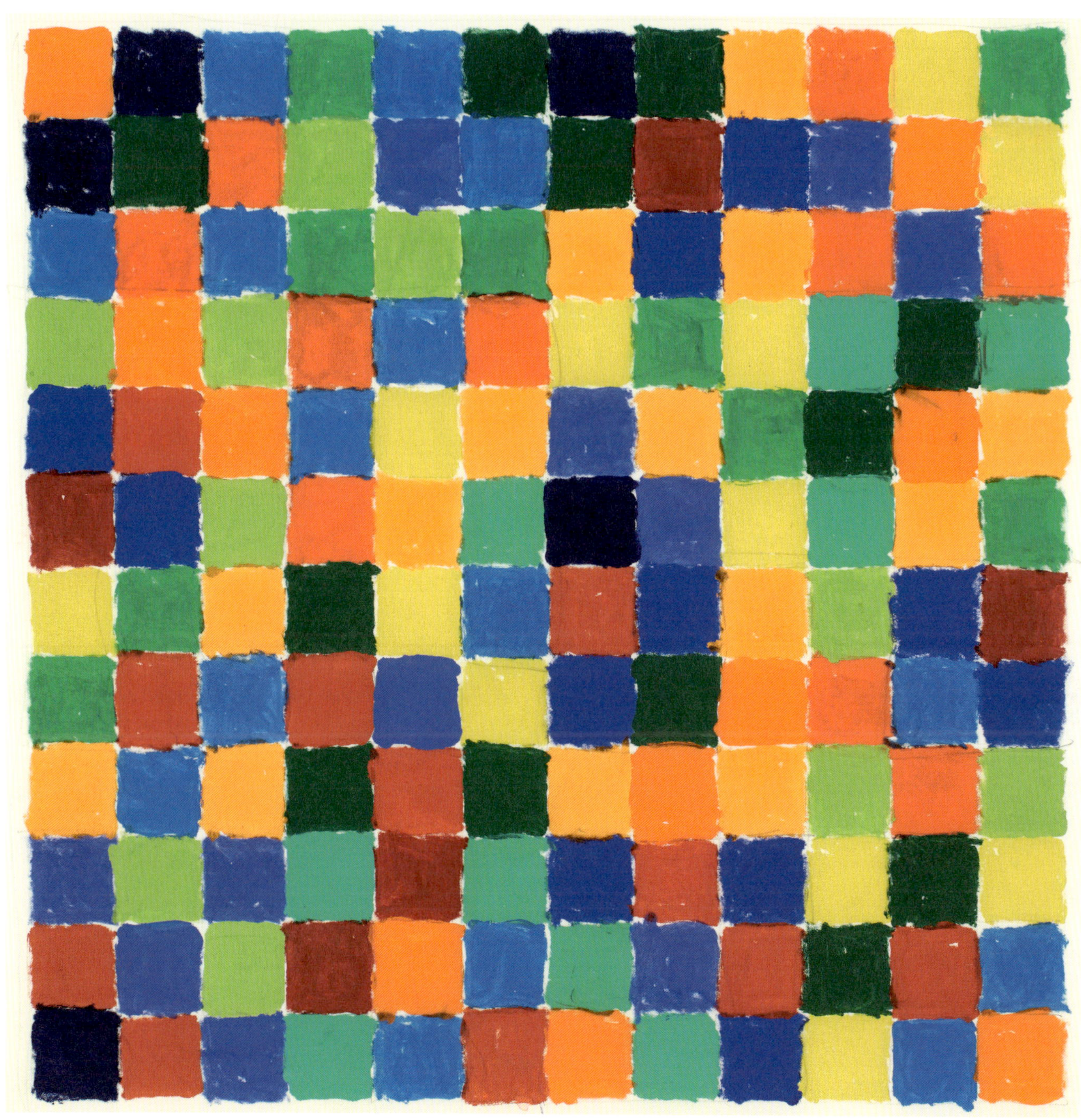

Cross, 1977, gouache on paper, 10 × 10 inches

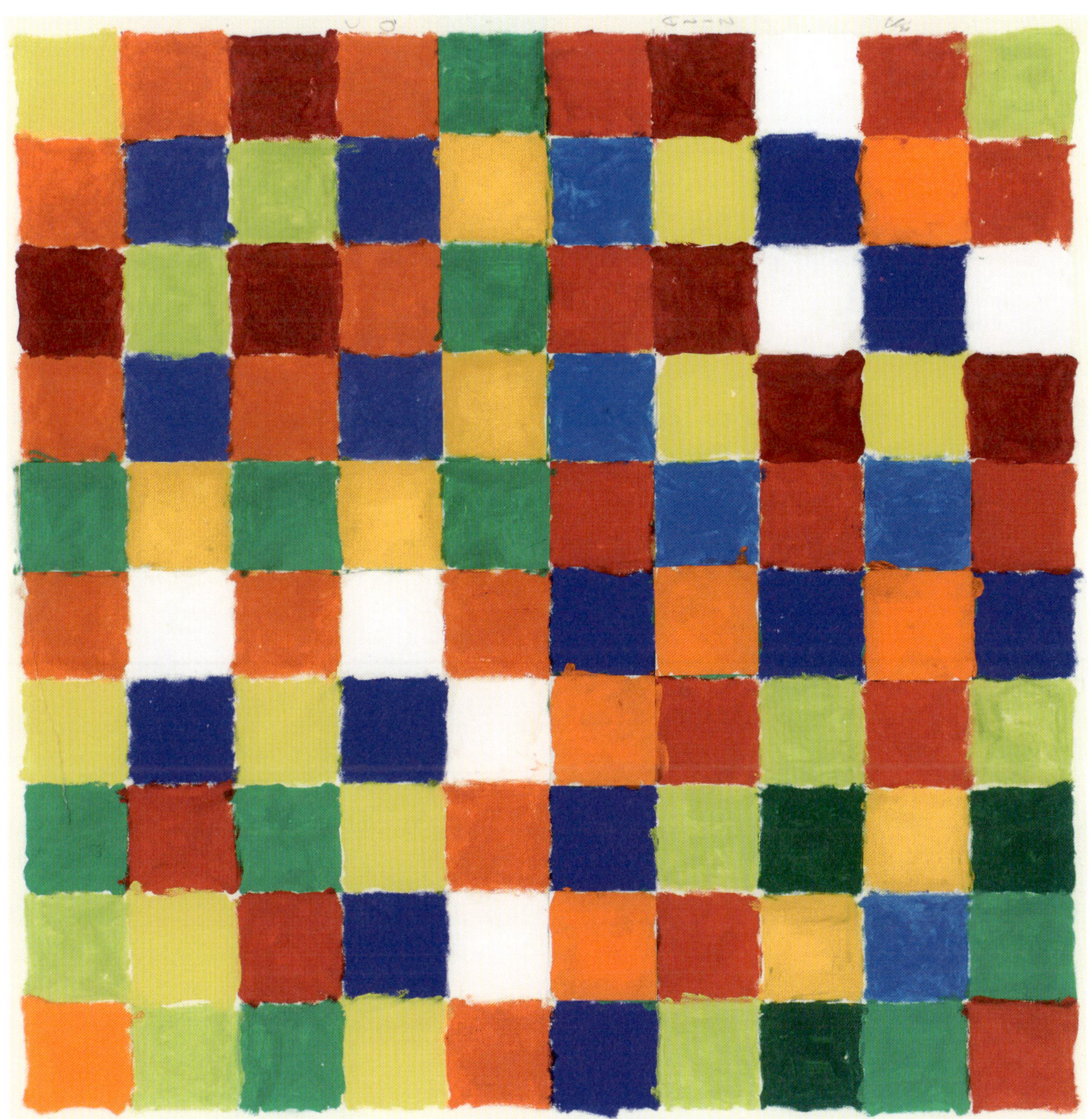

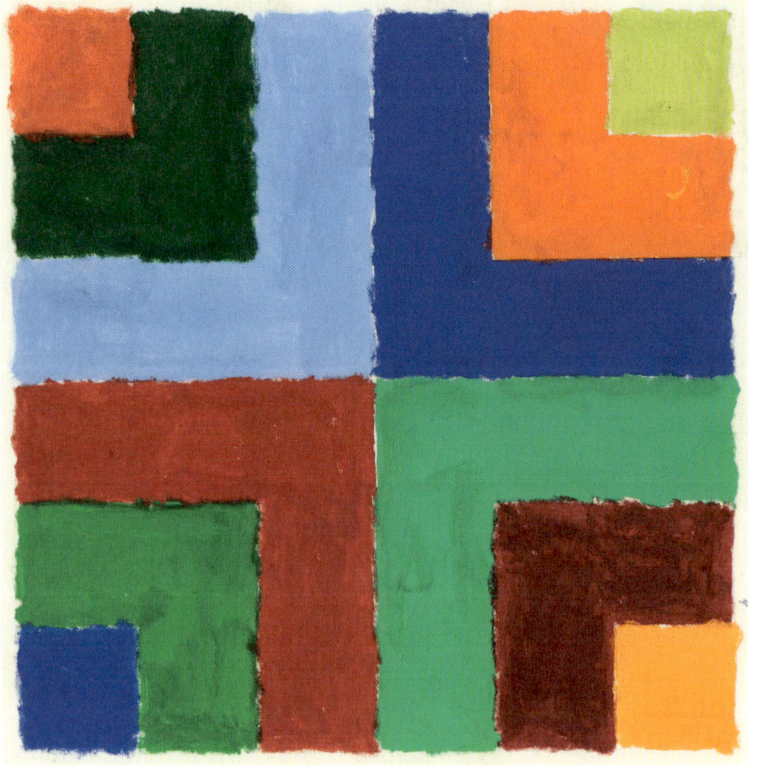

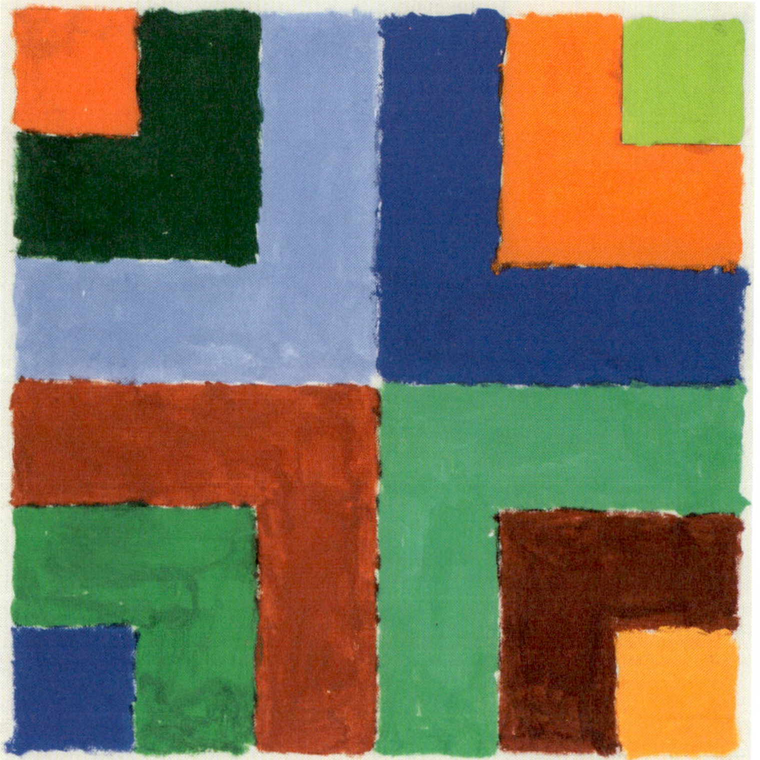

Cross, 1978, gouache on paper, 6 × 6 inches

Cross, 1978, gouache on paper, 6 × 6 inches

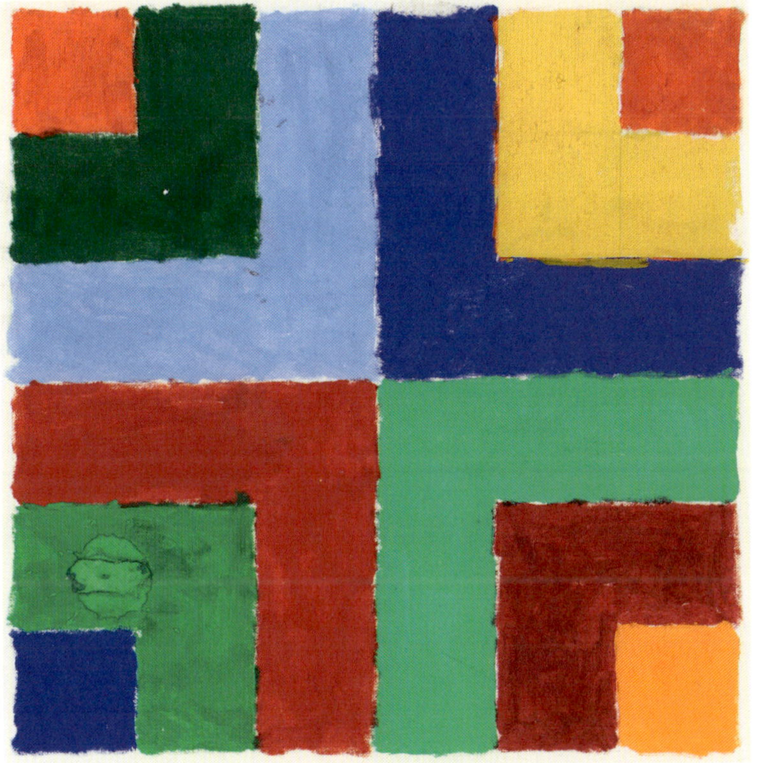

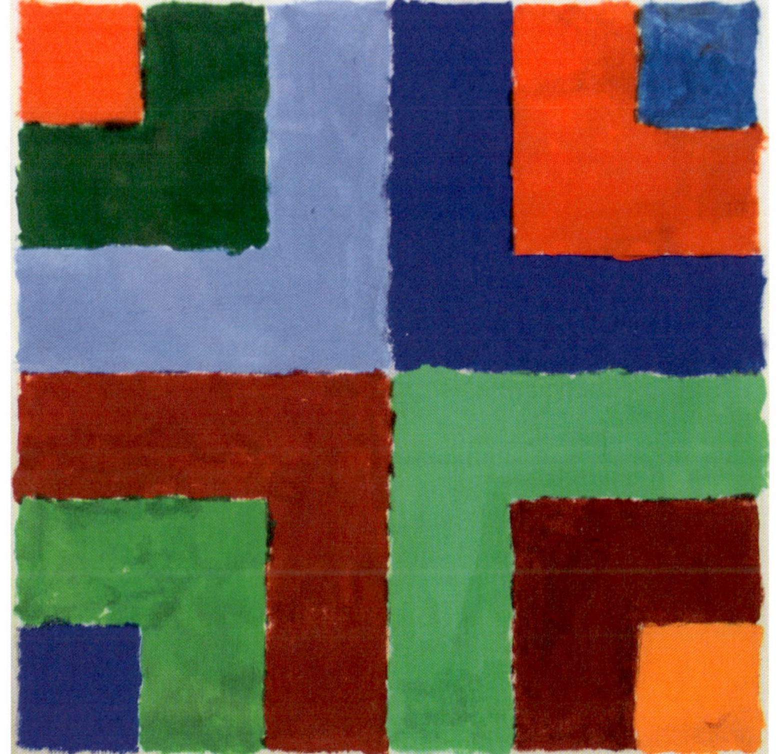

Cross, 1978, gouache on paper, 6 × 6 inches
Cross, 1978, gouache on paper, 6 × 6 inches

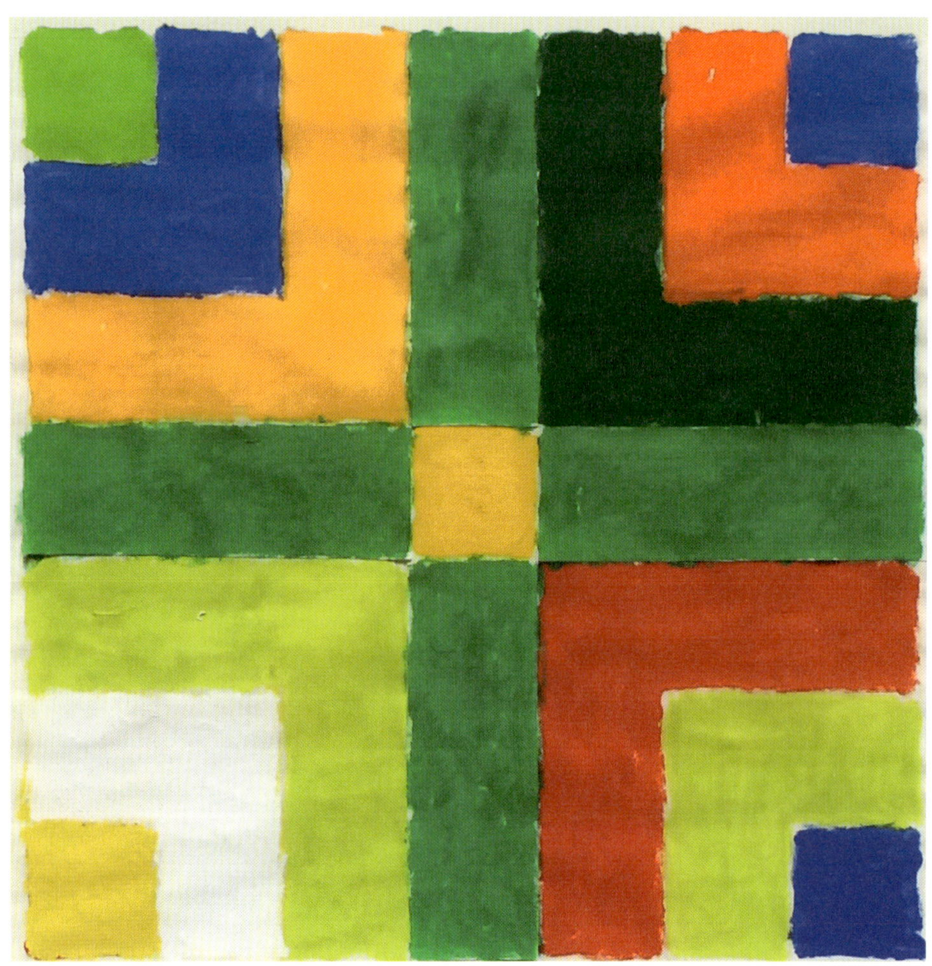

 Cross, 1978, gouache on paper, 7 × 7 inches

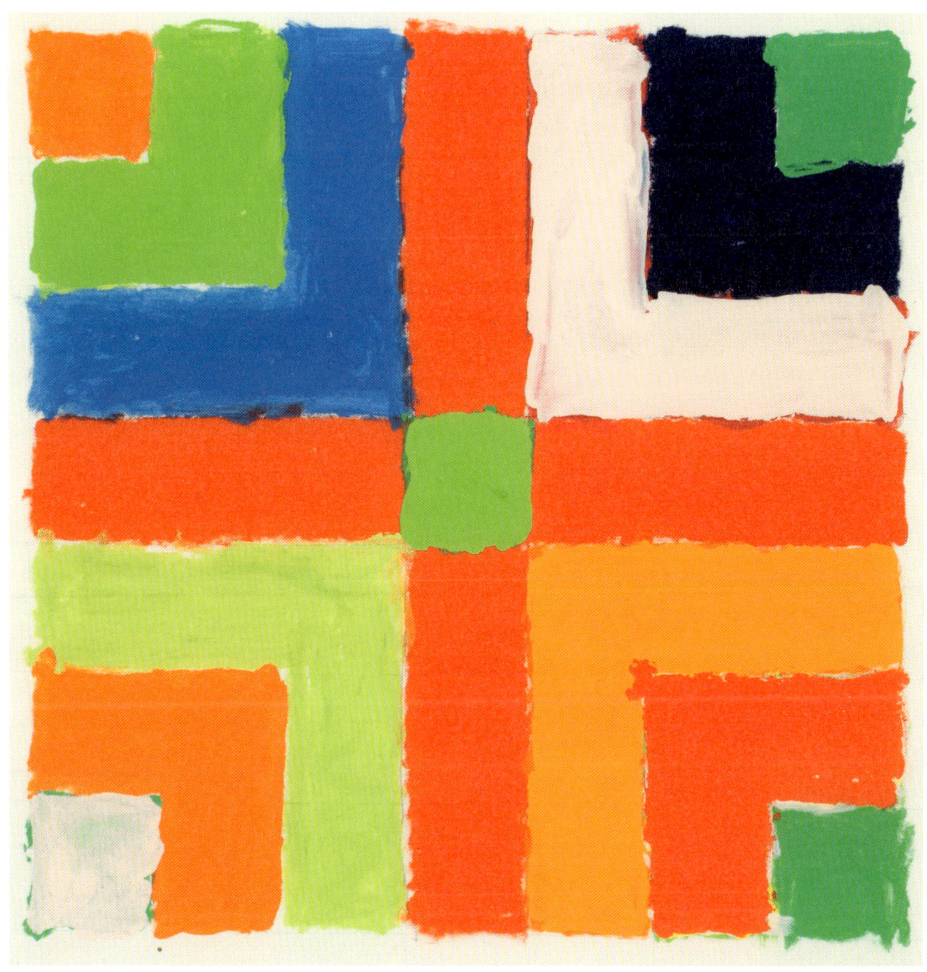

75 *Cross*, 1978, gouache on paper, 7 × 7 inches

Trees

Tree, 1977, gouache on paper, 21 × 15 inches

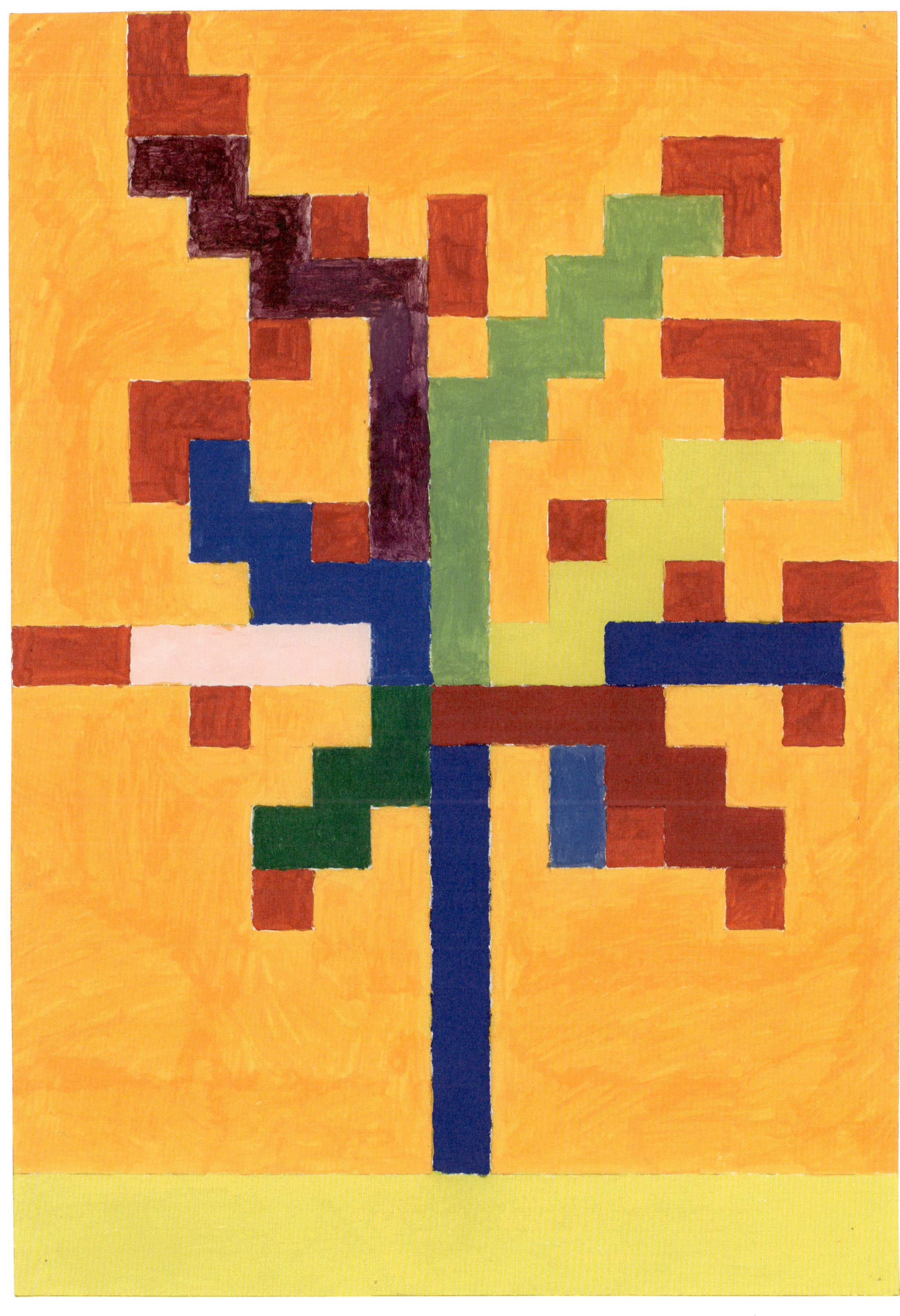

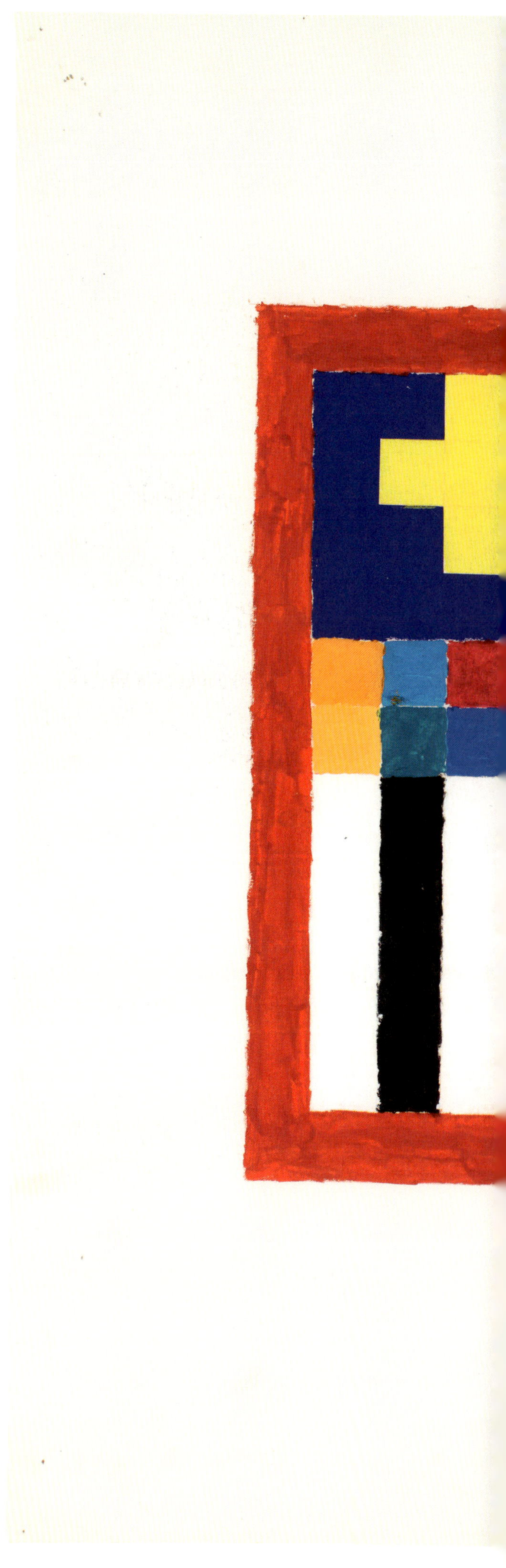

 Landscape, 1977, gouache on paper, 22½ × 28 inches

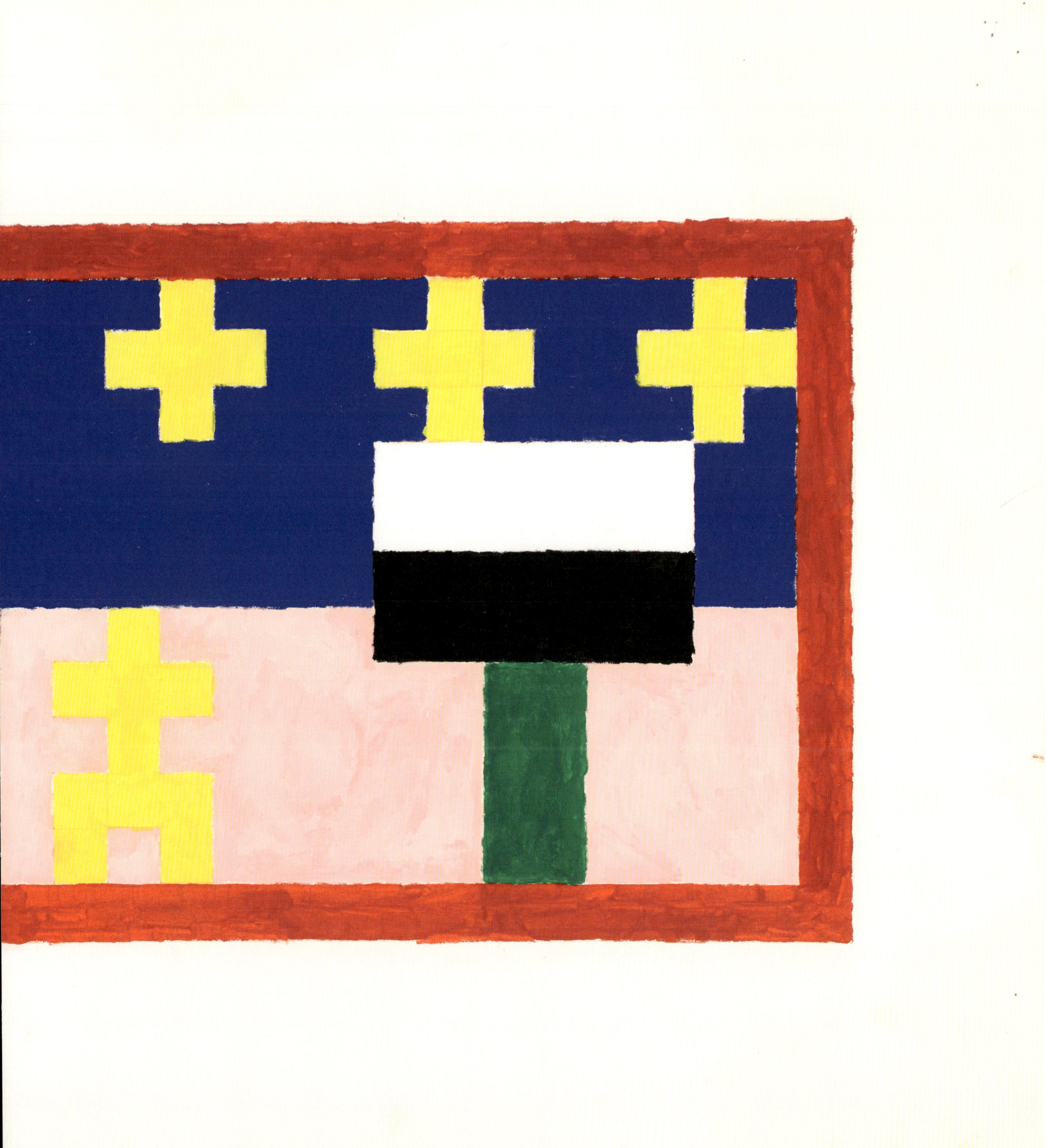

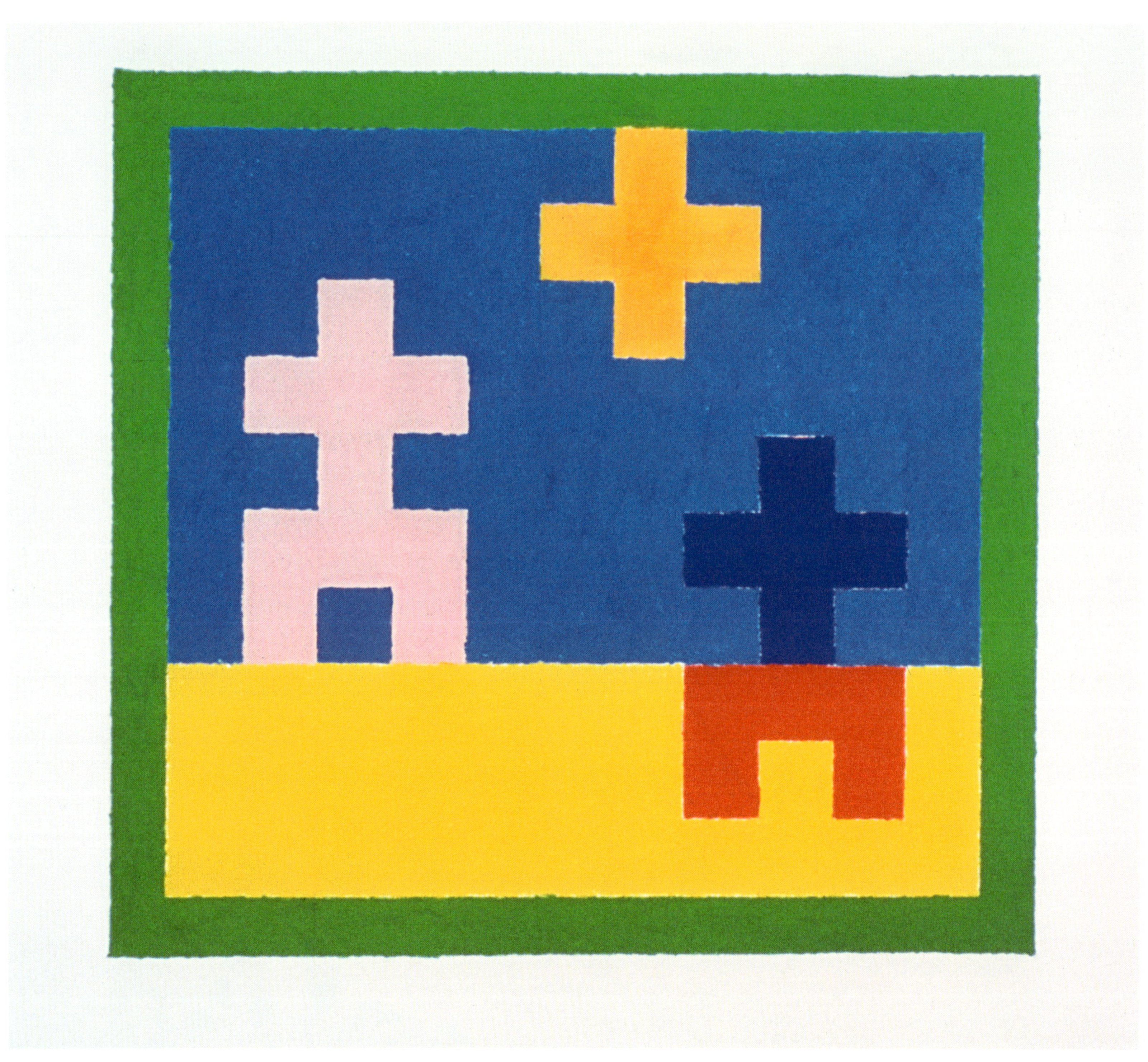

 Man Tree and Star, 1977, gouache on paper, 30 × 32 inches

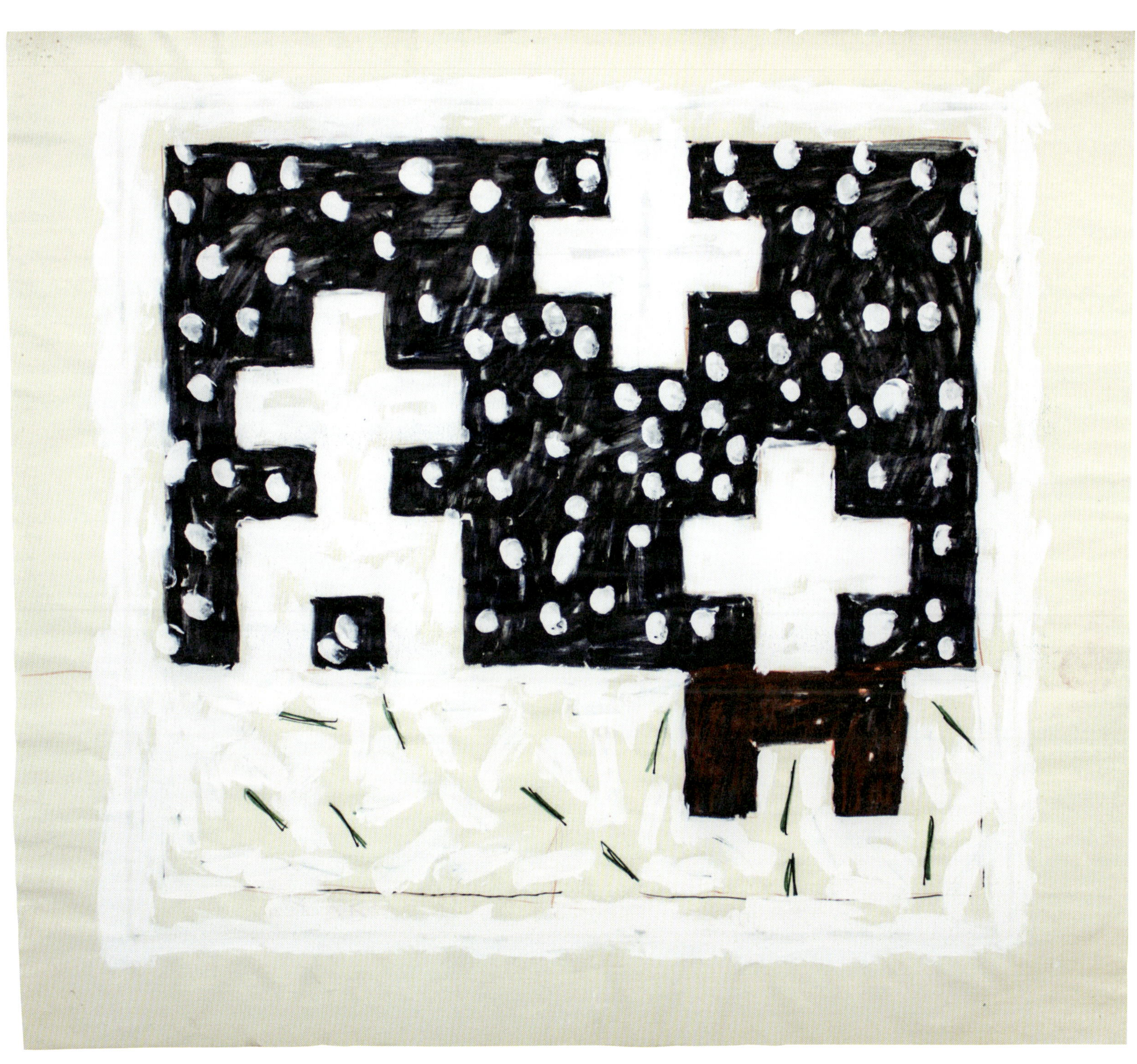

 Man Tree and Star, 1977, gouache and pencil on paper, 30 × 32 inches

Tree in a Landscape, 1977, gouache and pencil on paper, 10¾ × 8¾ inches

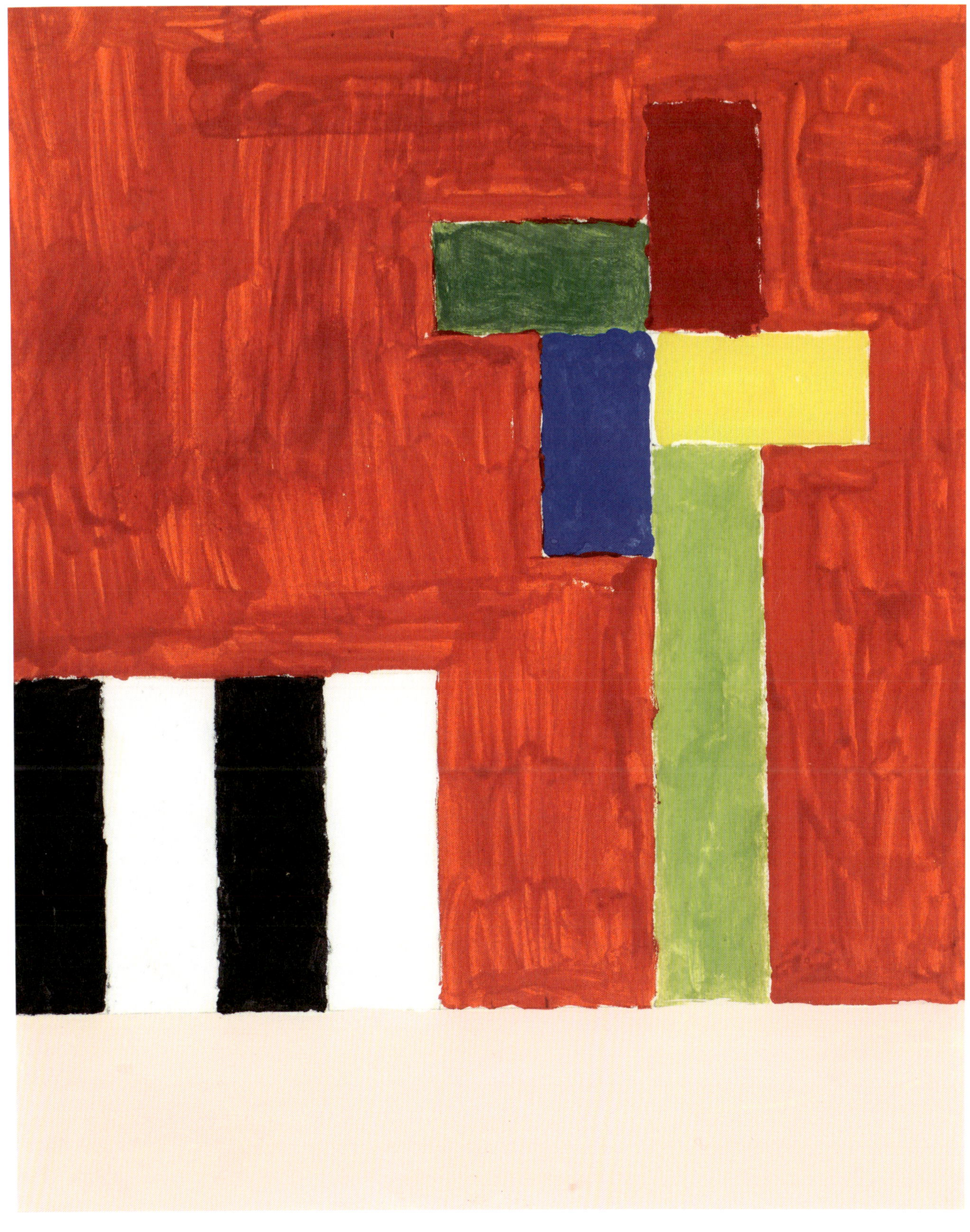

 Tree and Sun, 1977, gouache and pencil on paper, 8½ × 11 inches

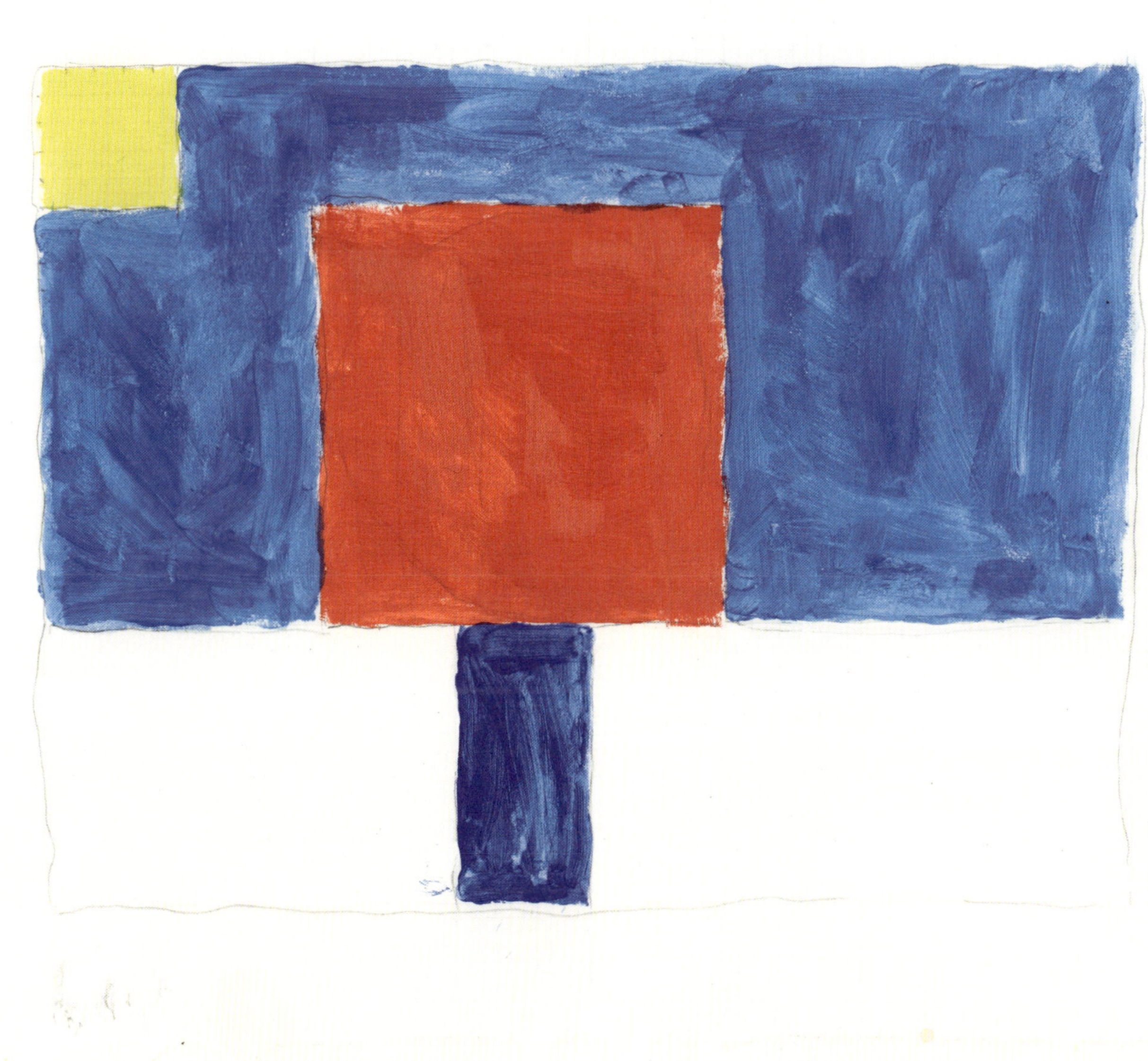

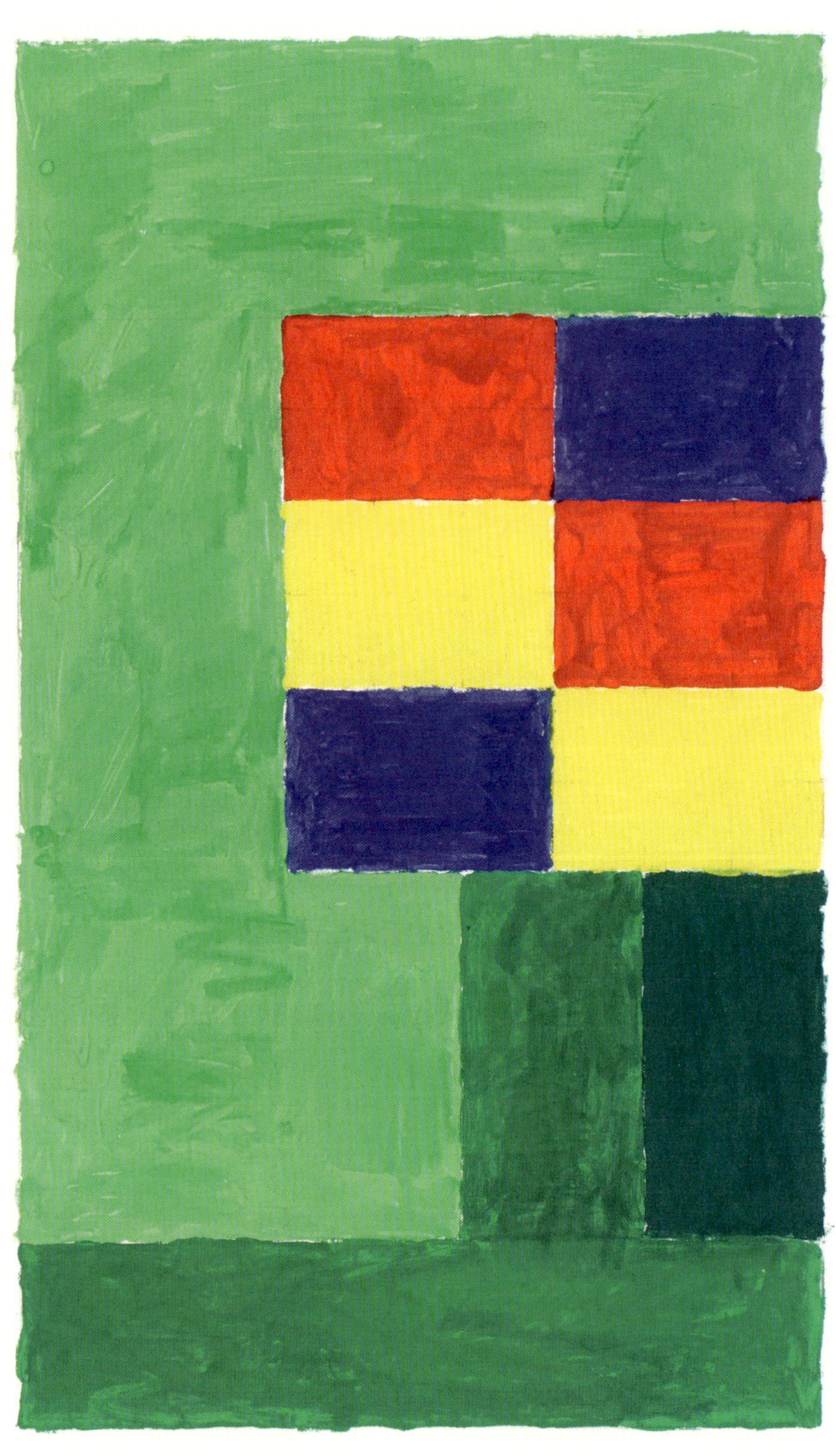

 Tree, 1977, gouache and pencil on paper, 28 × 22½ inches

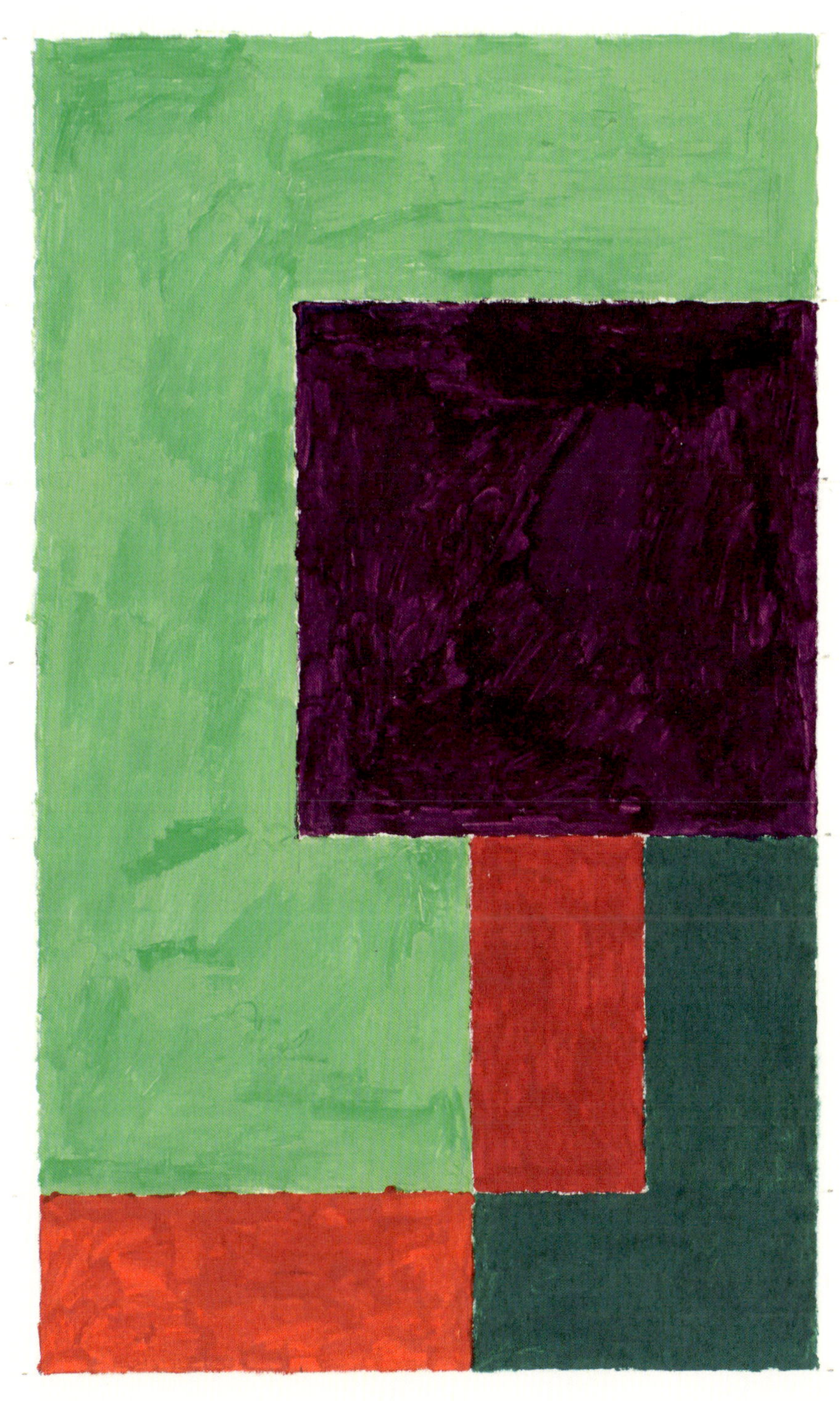

89 *Tree*, 1977, gouache and pencil on paper, 28 × 22½ inches

 Landscape with Two Trees, 1977, gouache and pencil on paper, 17 × 20 inches

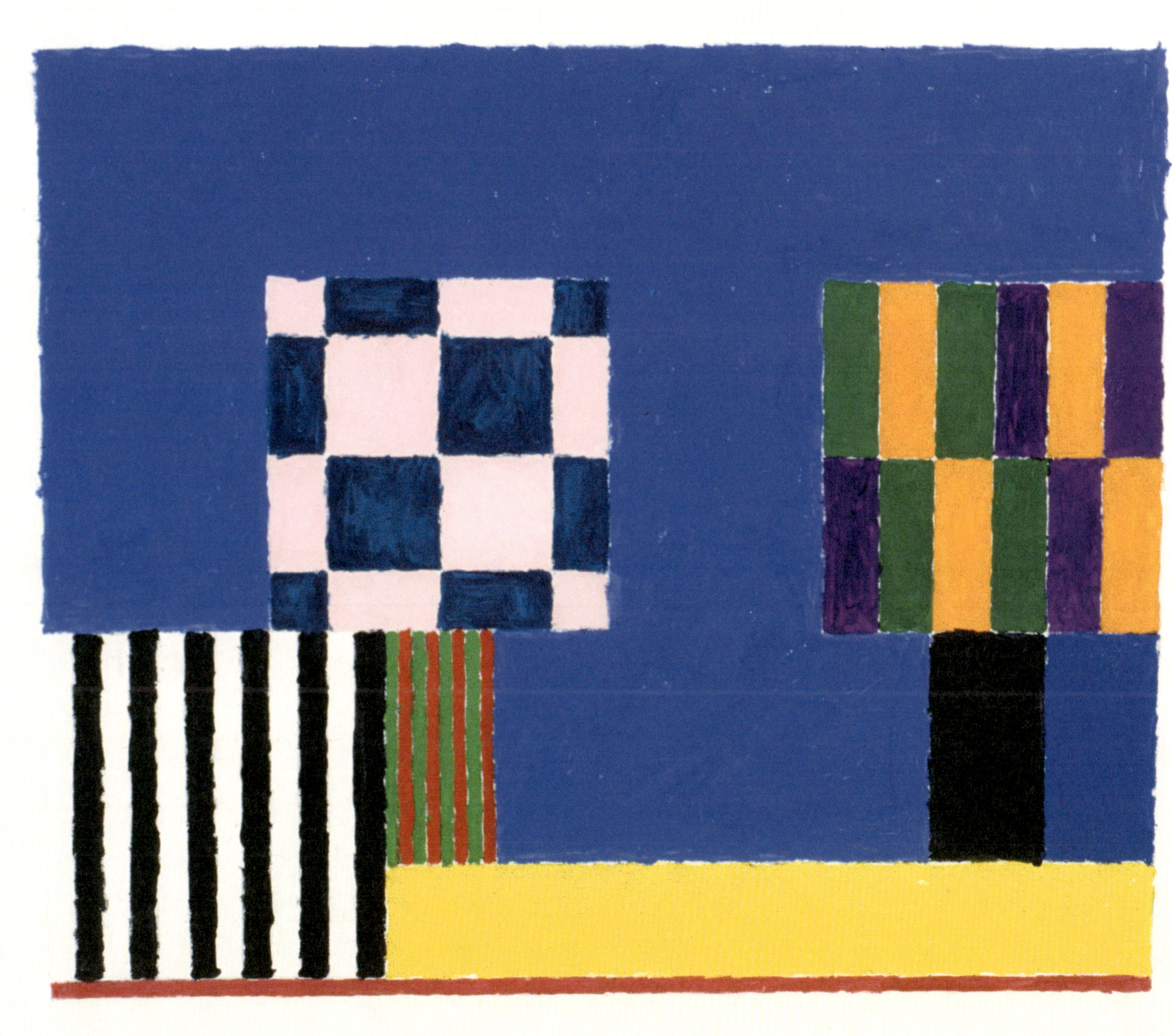

Tree, 1977, gouache and pencil on paper, 16¾ × 14 inches

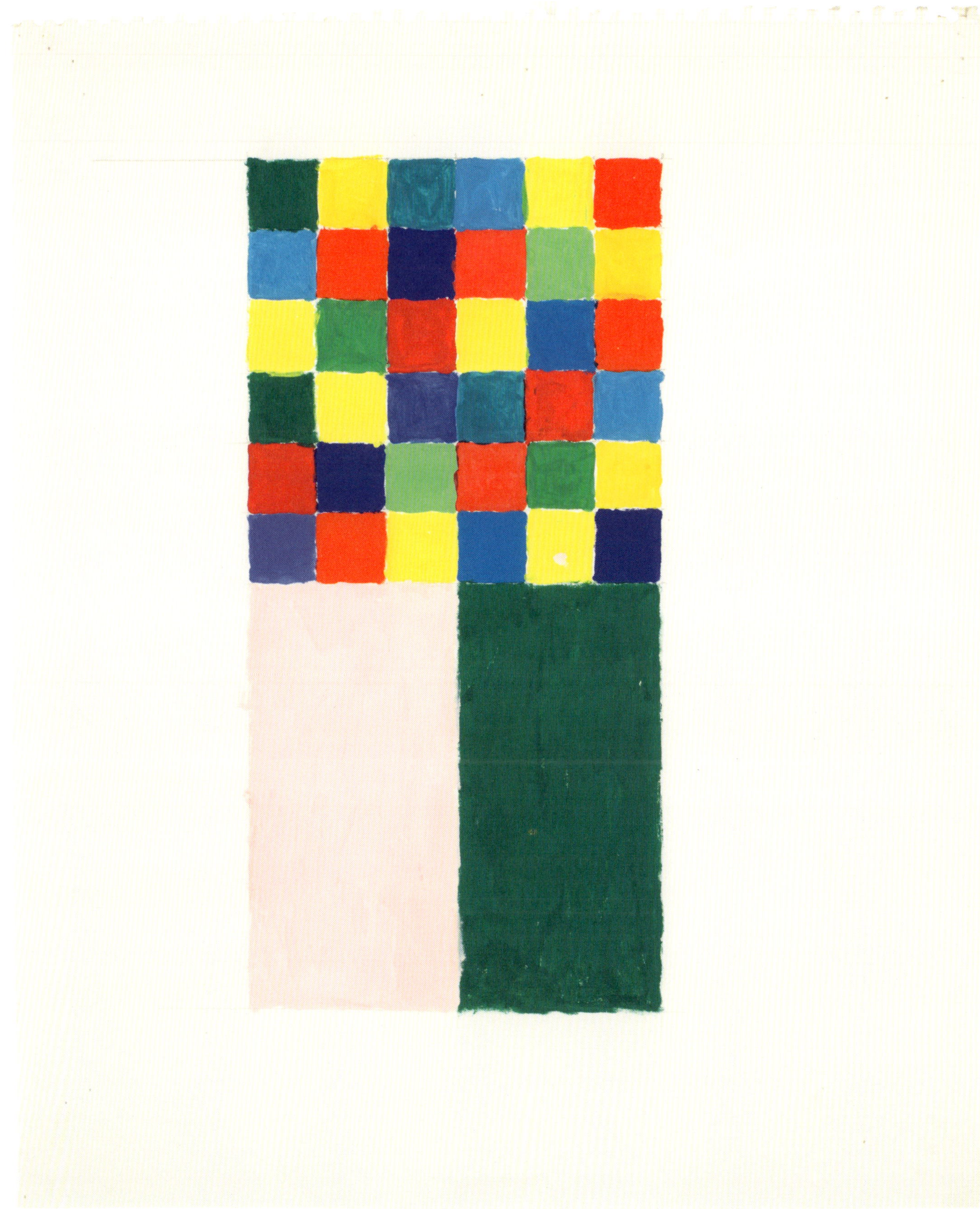

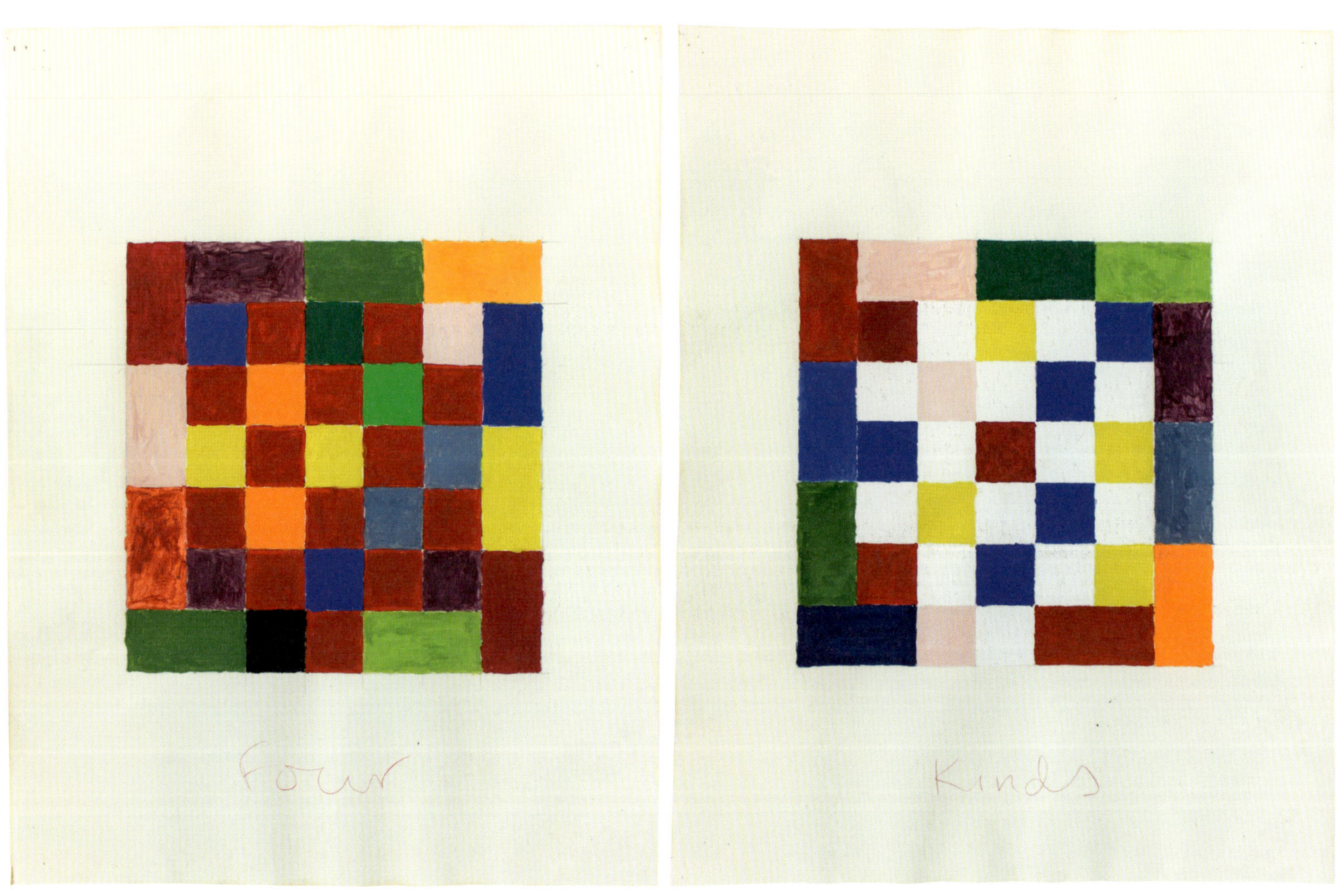

 Four Kinds of Trees, 1977, gouache and pencil on paper, 28 × 20 inches each

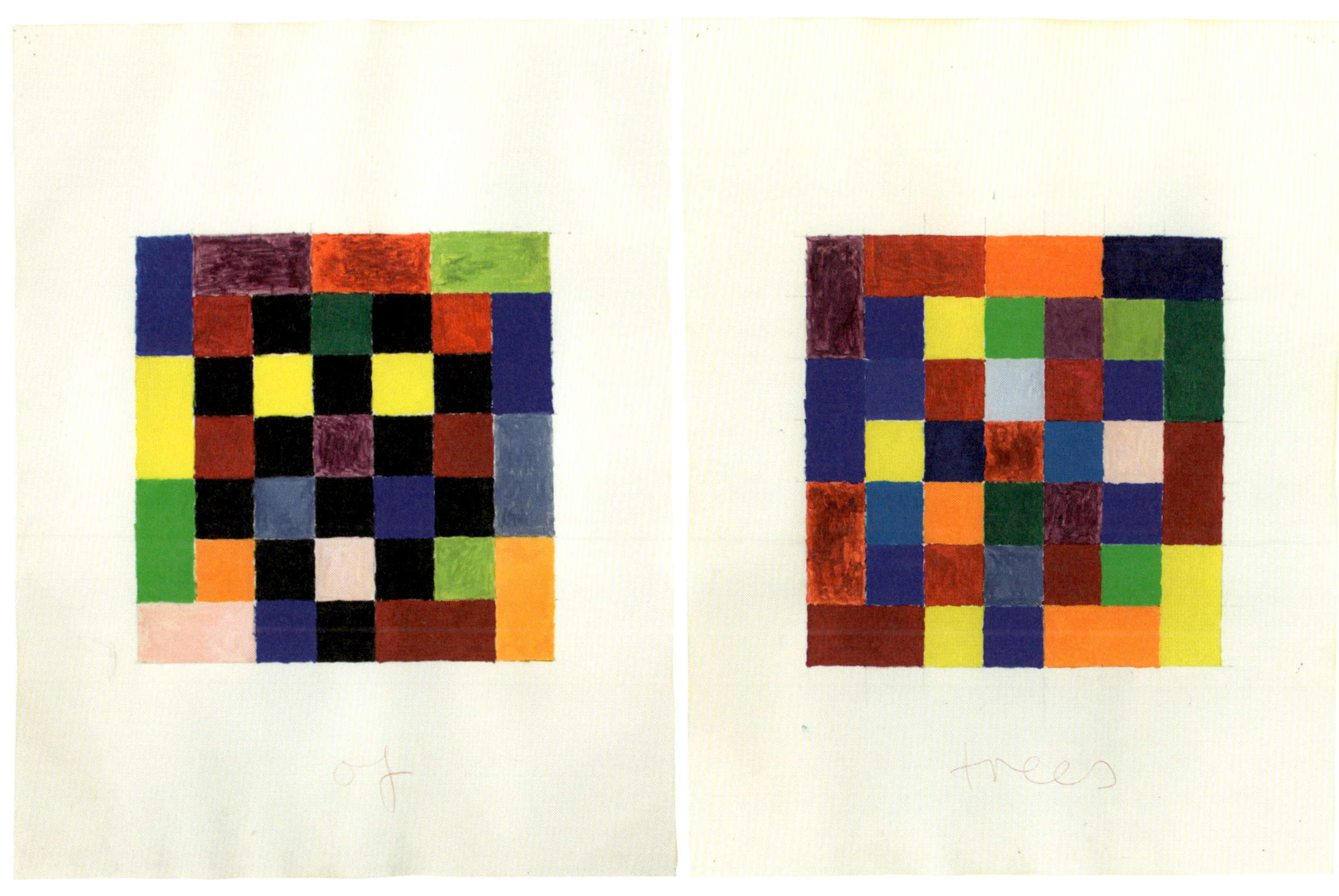
of
trees

 Trees, 1978, gouache and pencil on paper, 28 × 22 inches

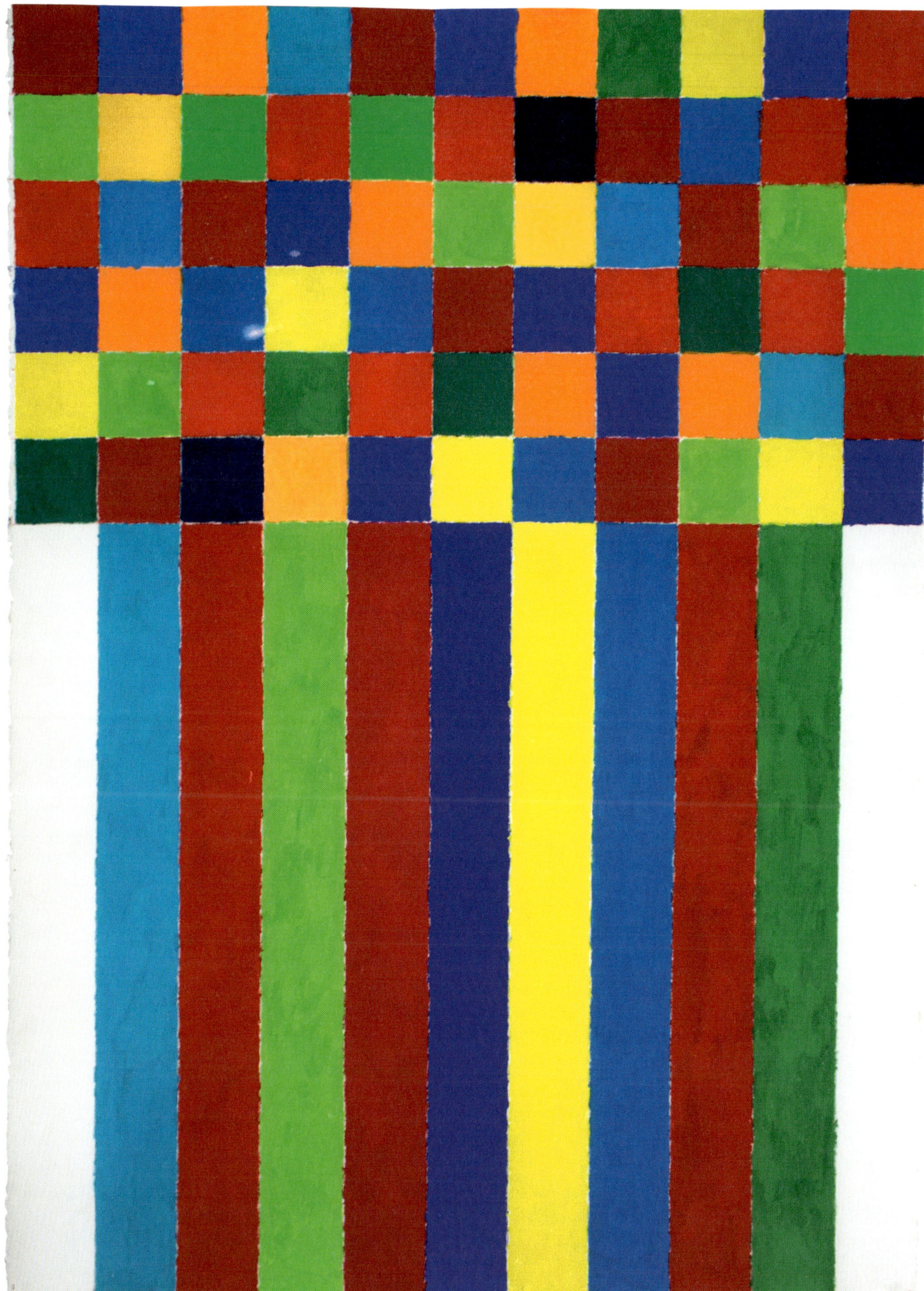

 Landscape with Trees, 1977, gouache and pencil on paper, 12 × 14 inches

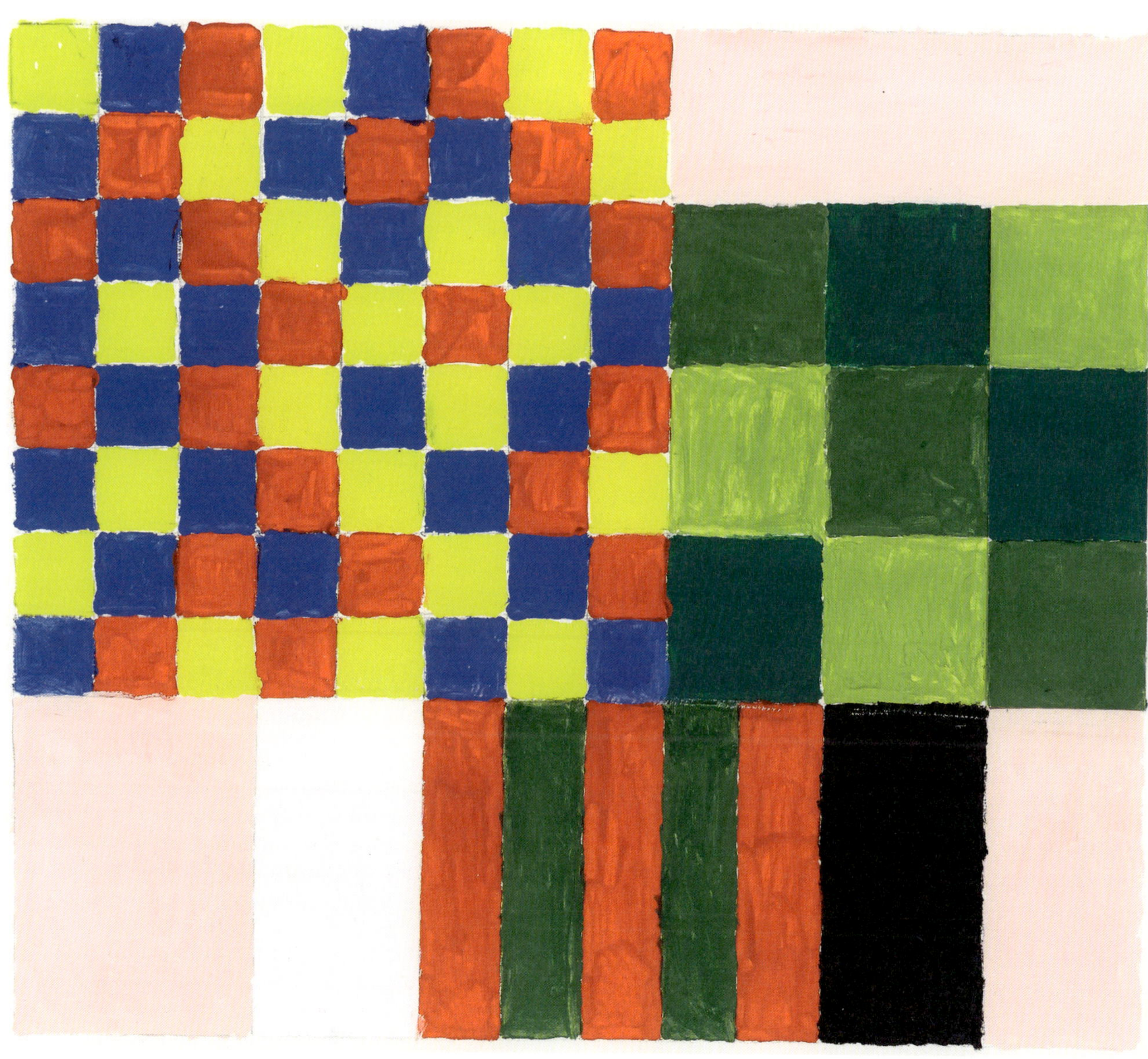

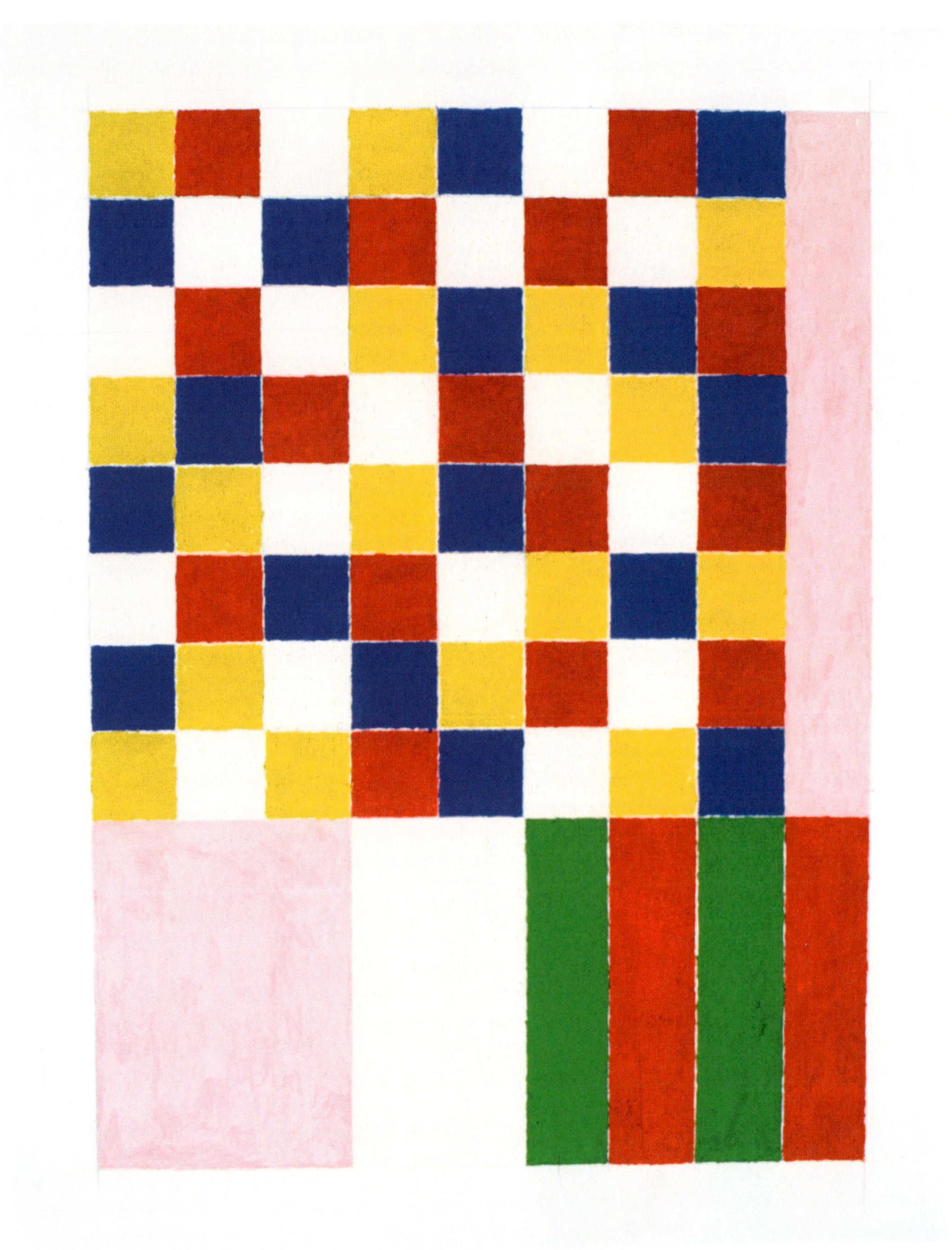

 Mondrian's Tree, 1978, gouache and pencil on paper, 30 × 24 inches

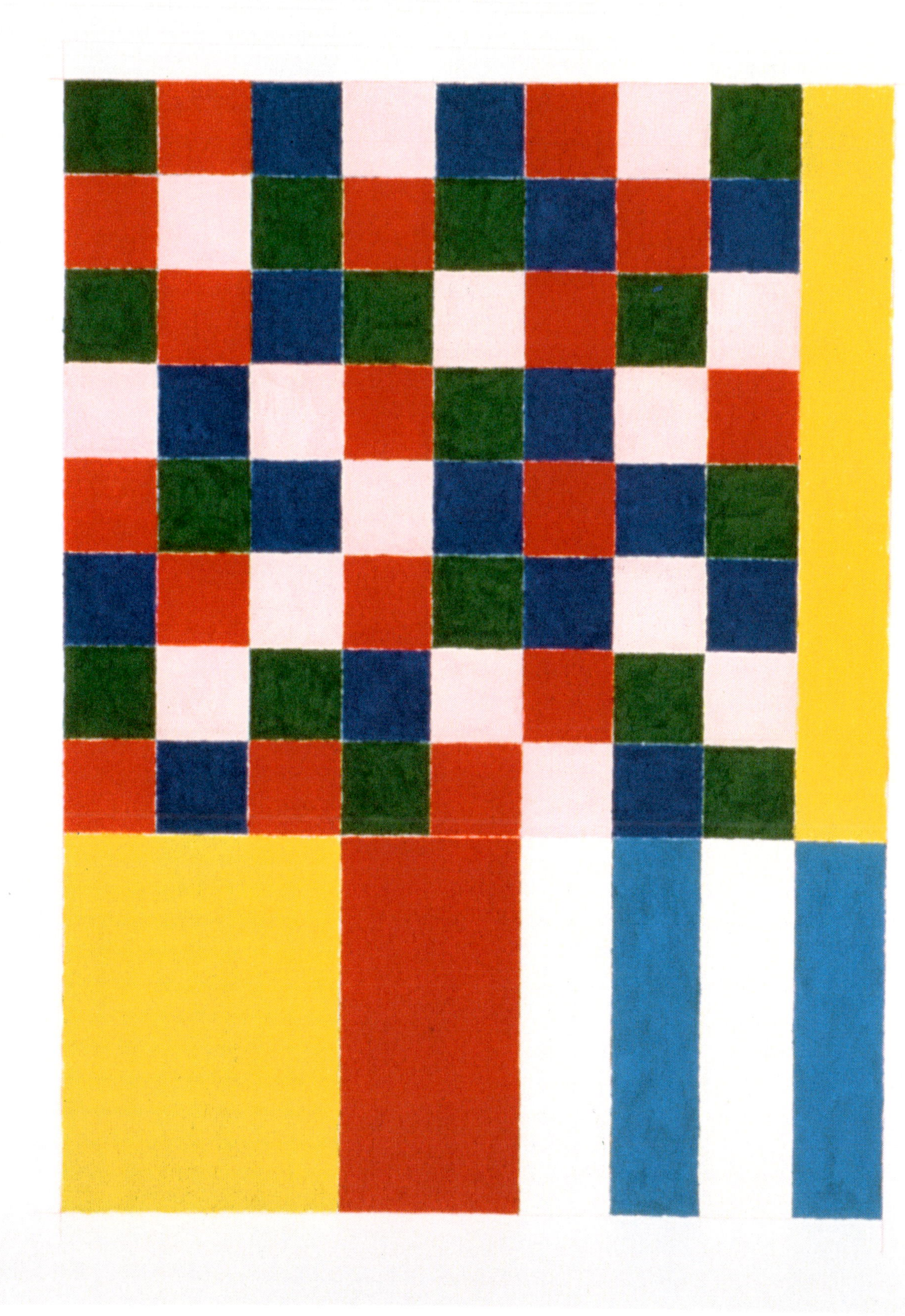

101 *An African Tree*, 1978, gouache and pencil on paper, 30 × 24 inches

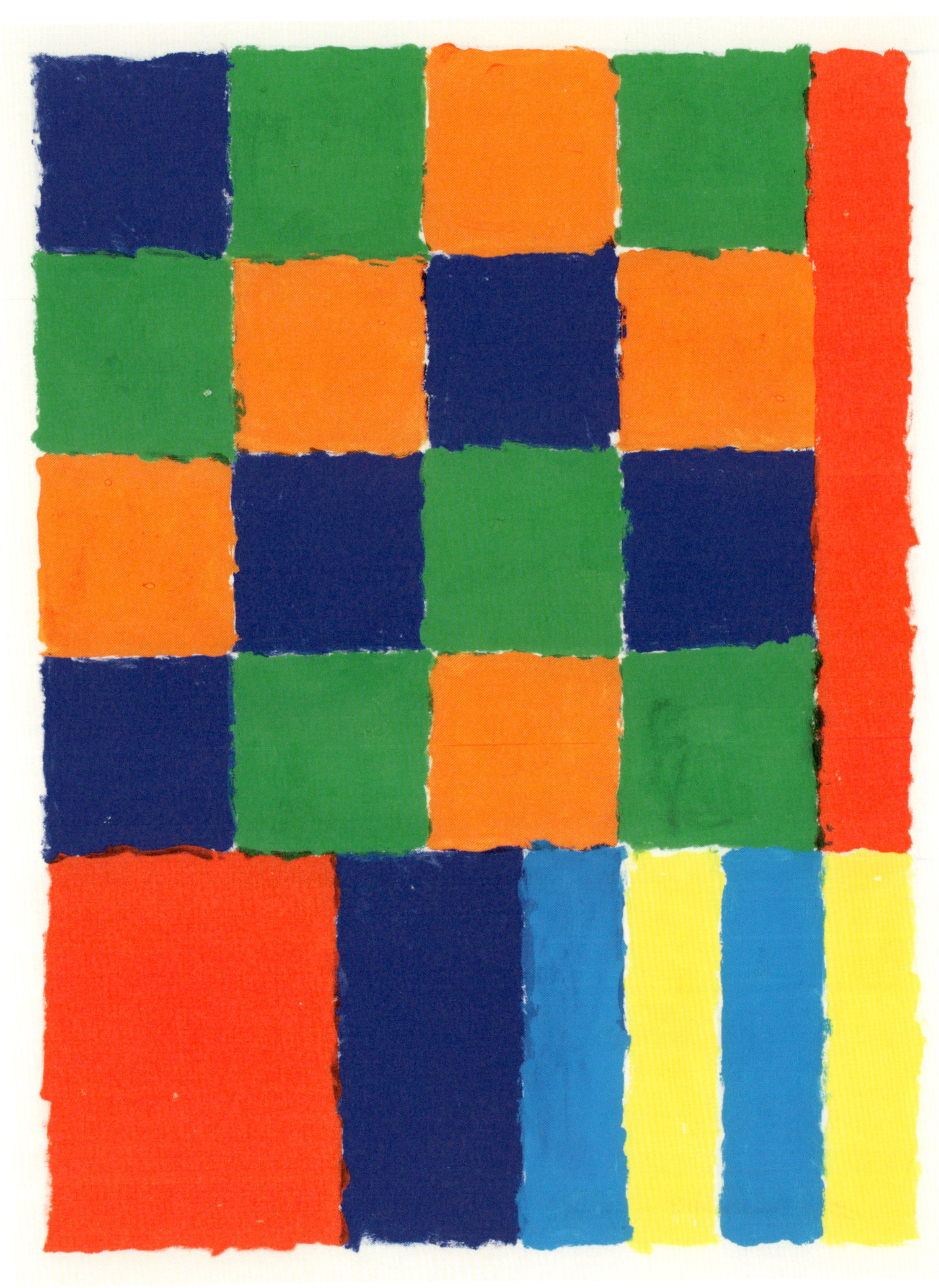

 Tree, 1978, gouache and pencil on paper, 12 × 9 inches

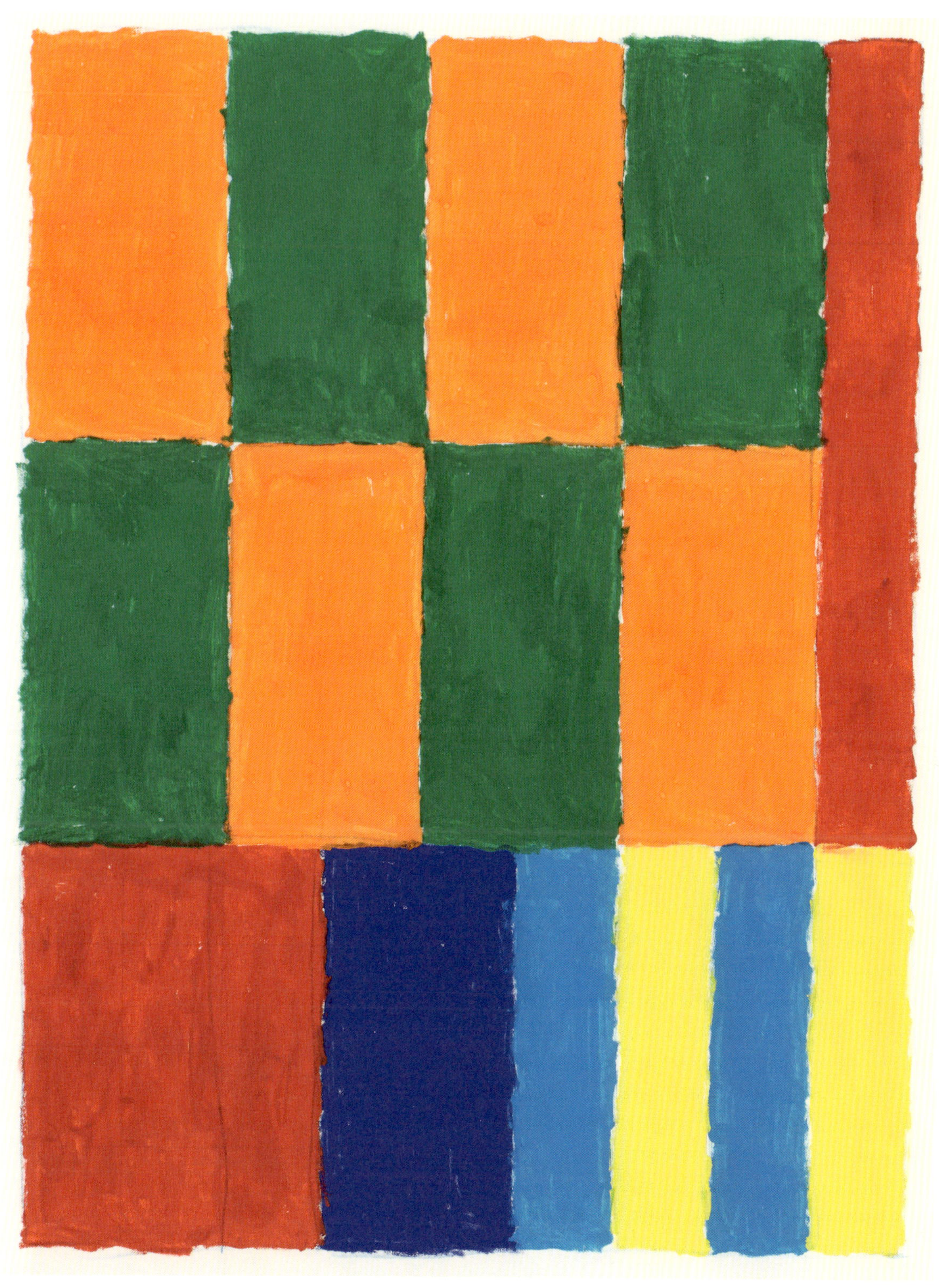

103 *Tree*, 1978, gouache and pencil on paper, 12 × 9 inches

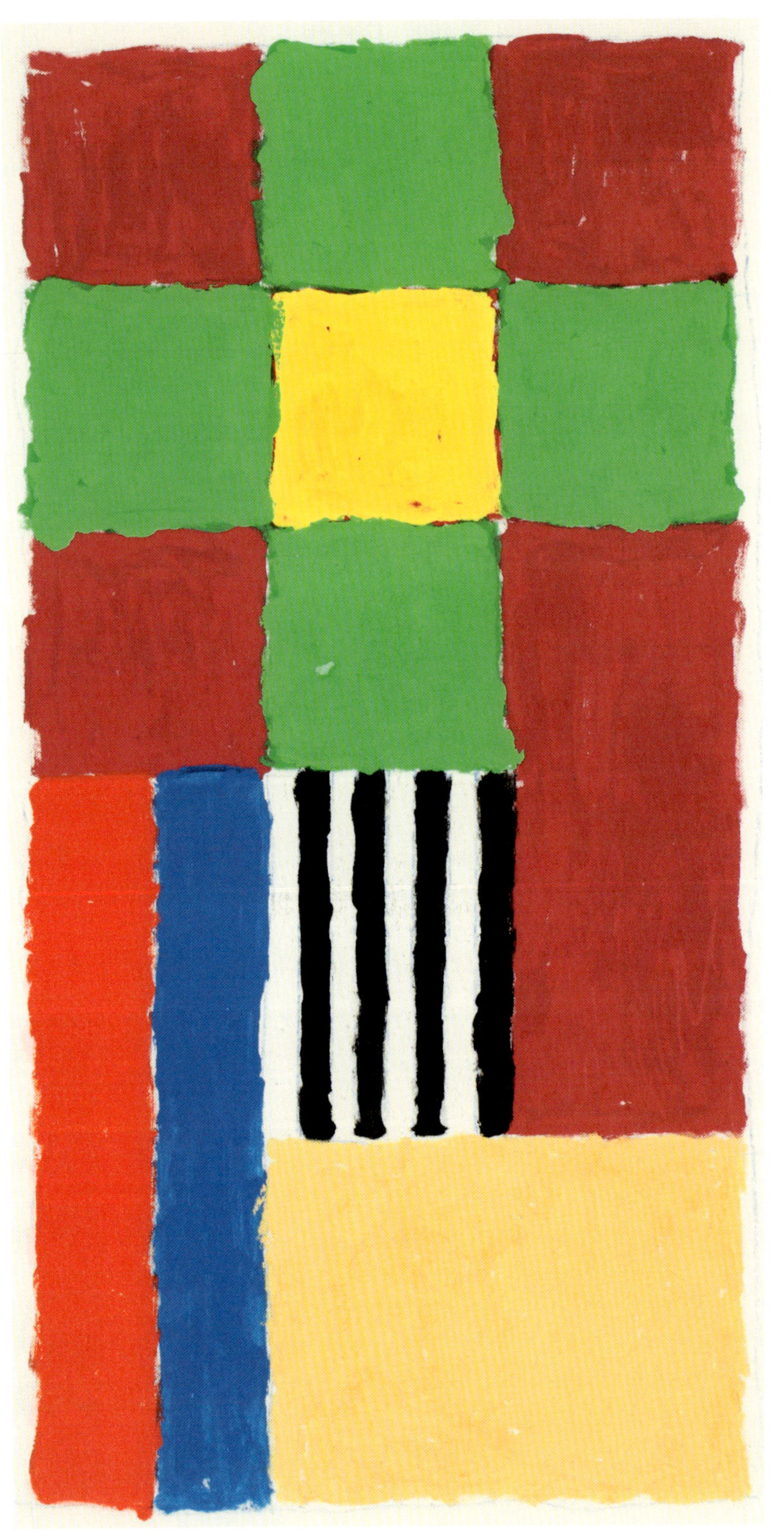

 Tree in a Landscape, 1978, gouache and pencil on paper, 12 × 6 inches

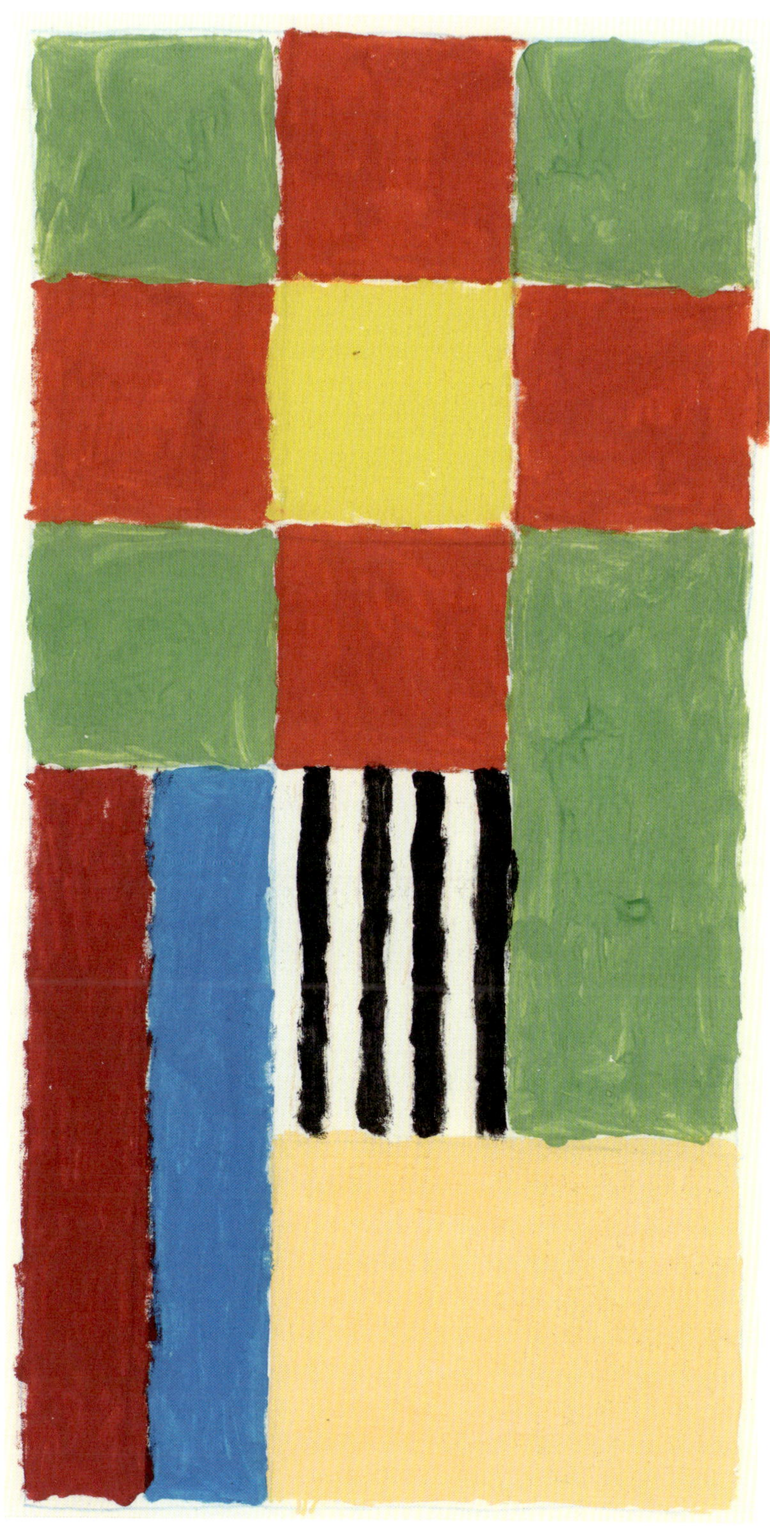

105 *Tree in a Landscape*, 1978, gouache and pencil on paper, 12 × 6 inches

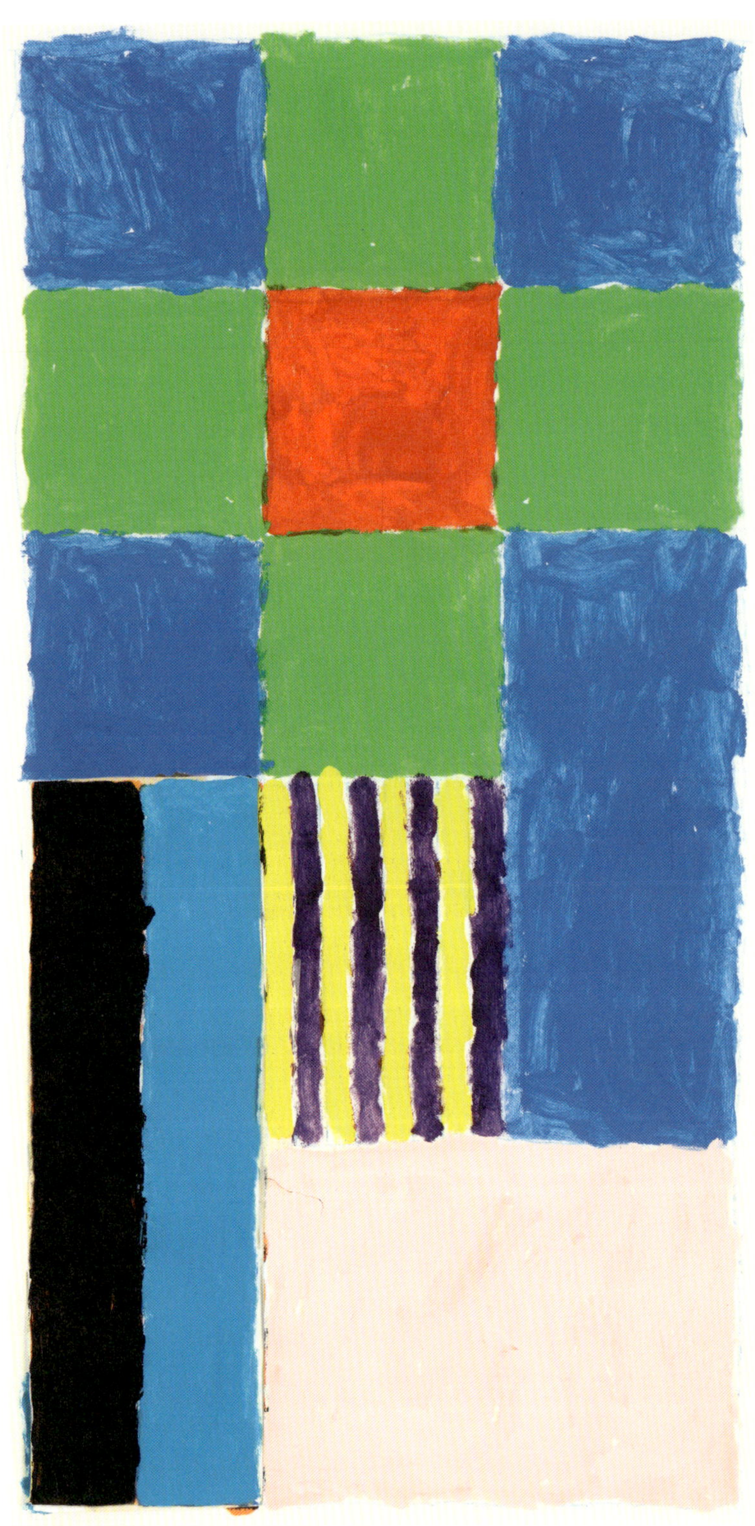

 Tree in a Landscape, 1978, gouache and pencil on paper with collage element, 12 × 6 inches

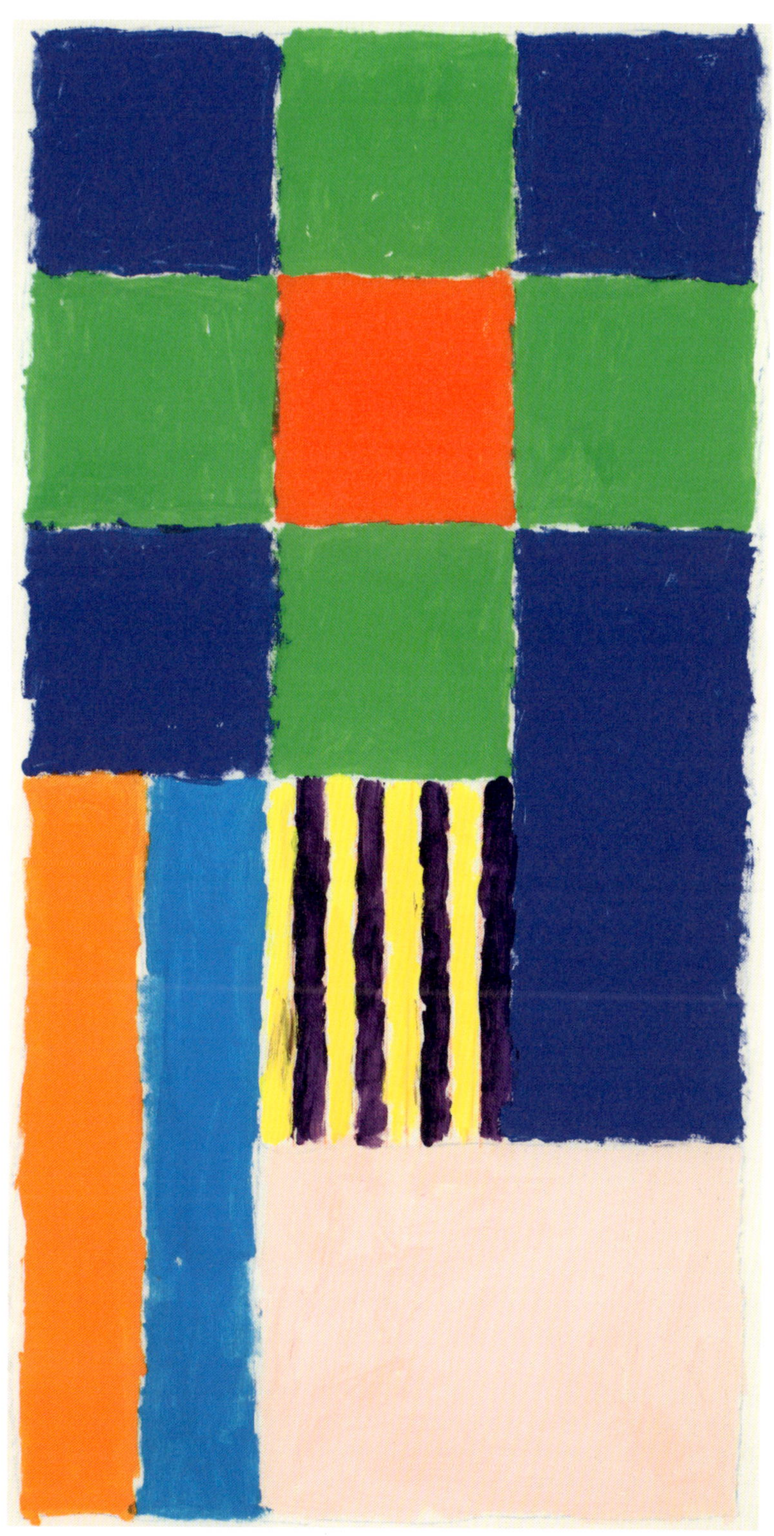

107 *Tree in a Landscape*, 1978, gouache and pencil on paper, 12 × 6 inches

 Tree in a Landscape, 1978, gouache and pencil on paper, 42 × 30 inches

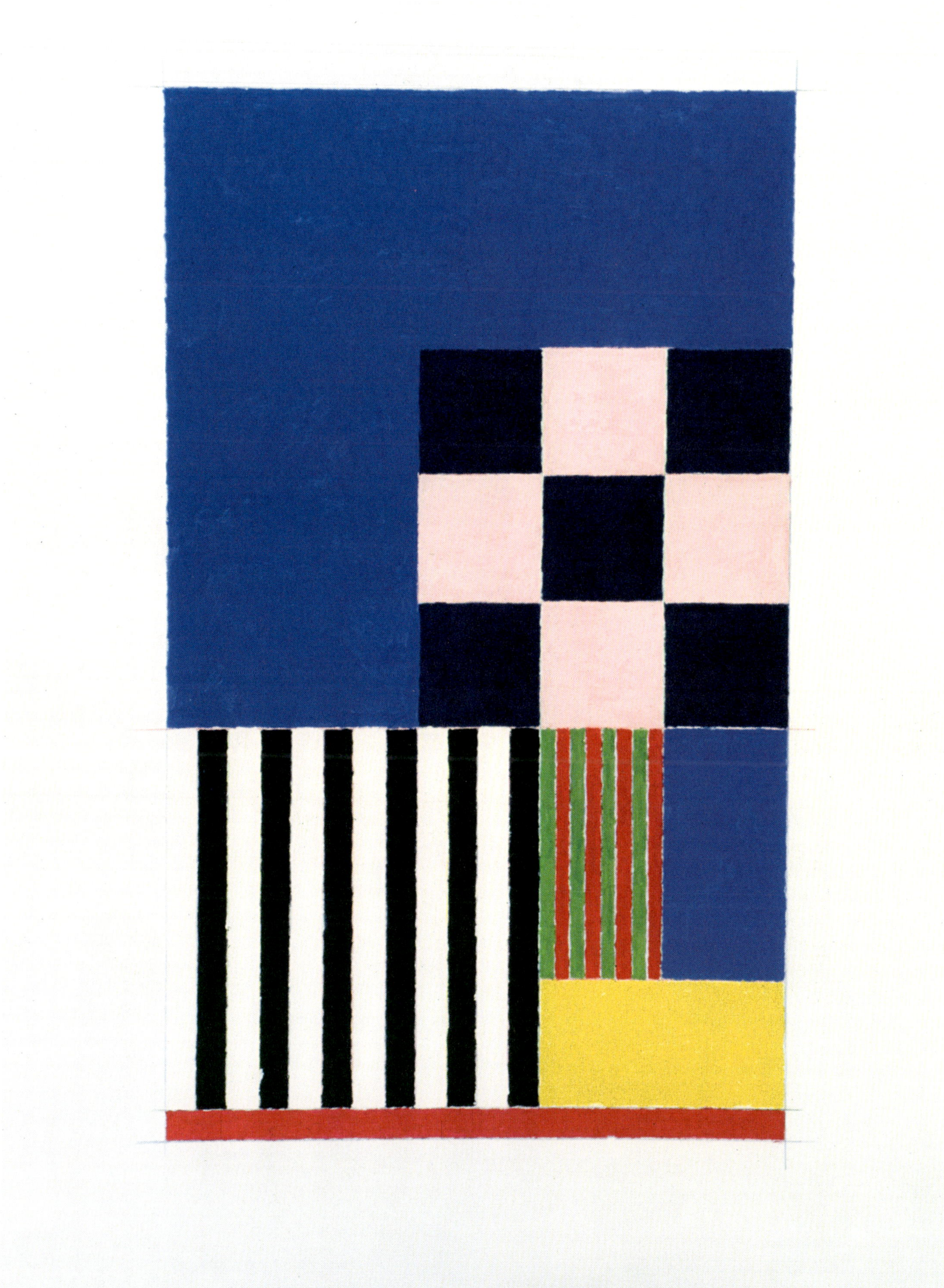

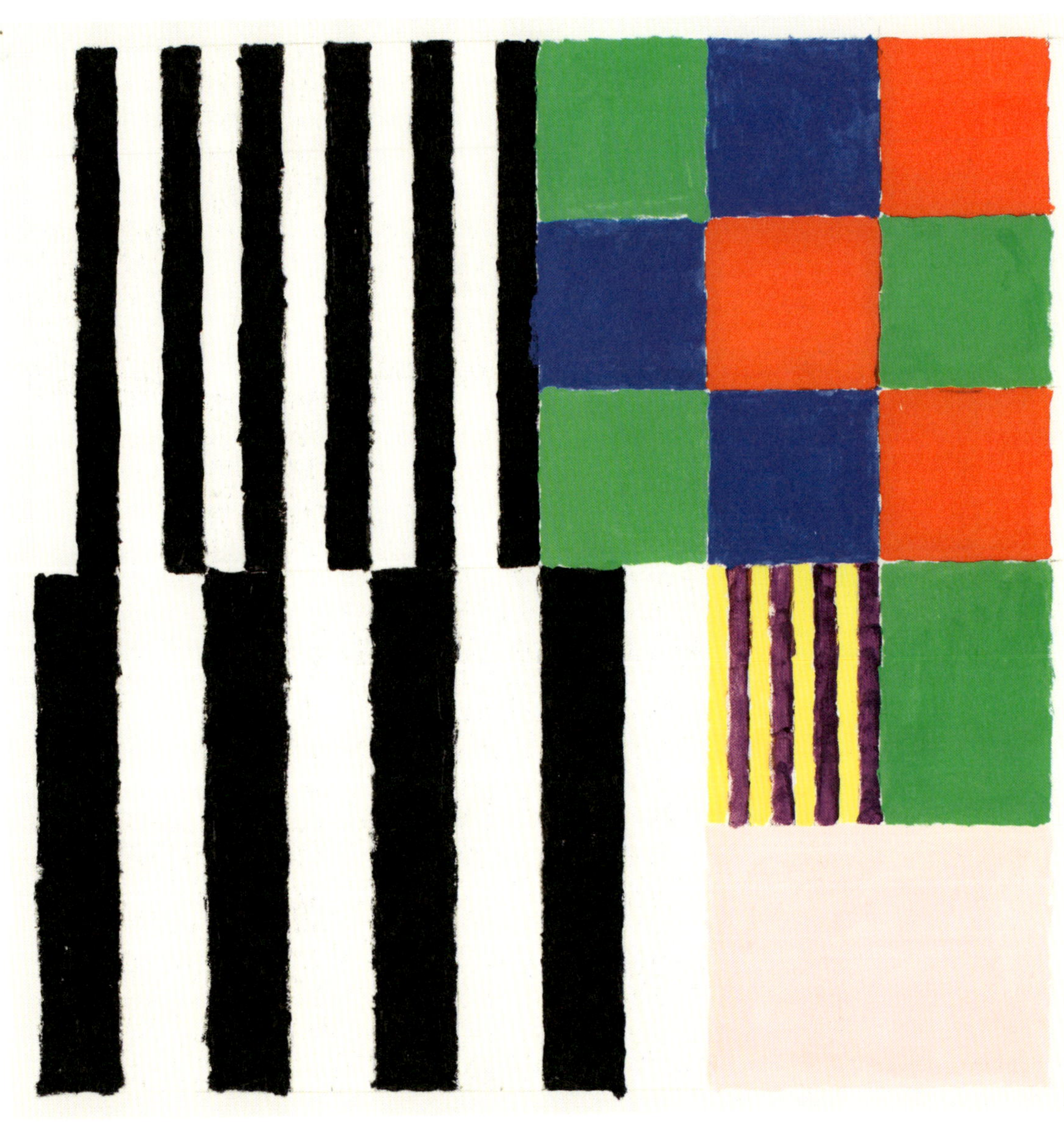

 Landscape with Tree, 1978, gouache and pencil on paper, 12 × 12 inches

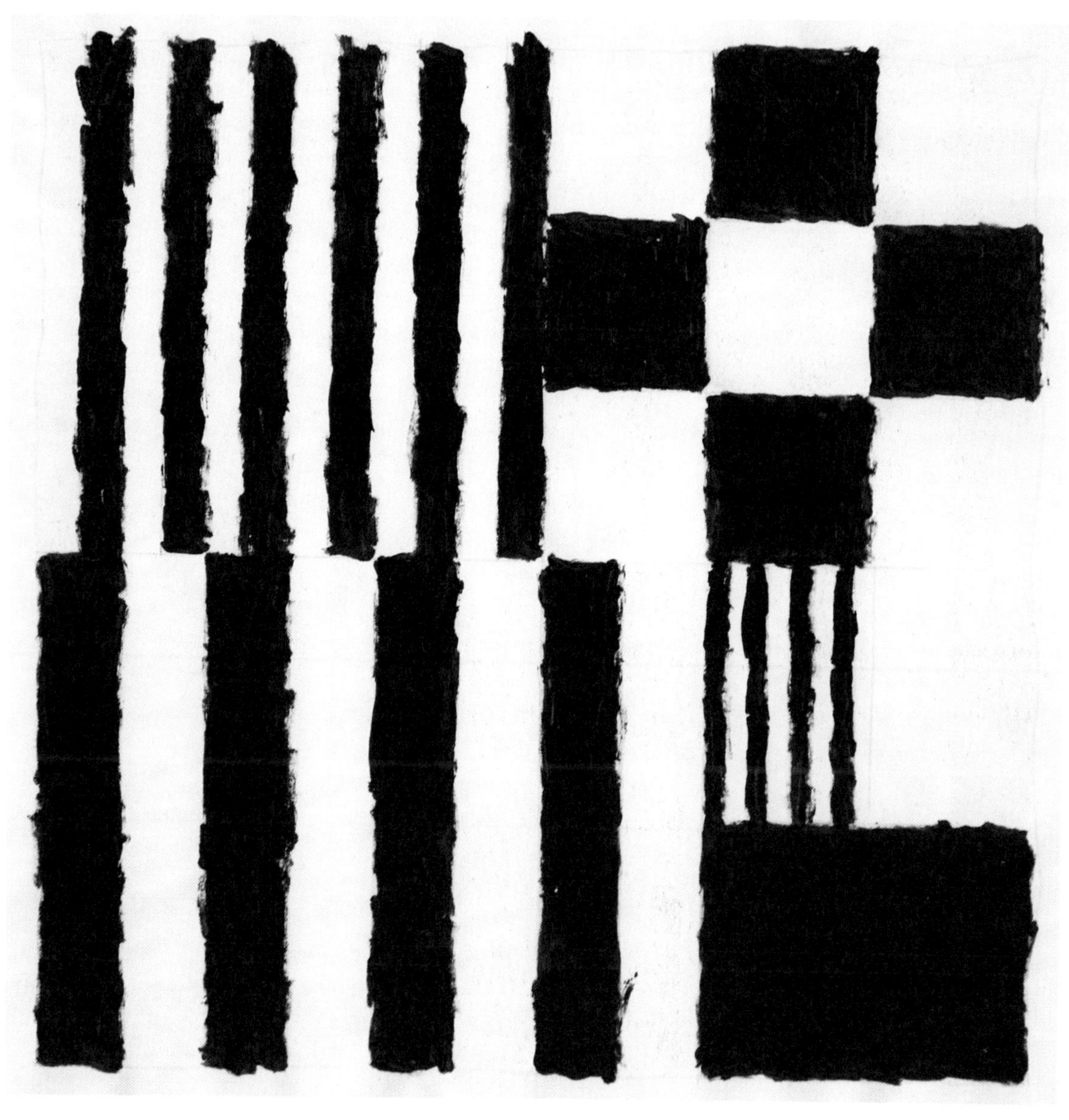

111 *Landscape with Tree*, 1978, gouache and pencil on paper, 12 × 12 inches

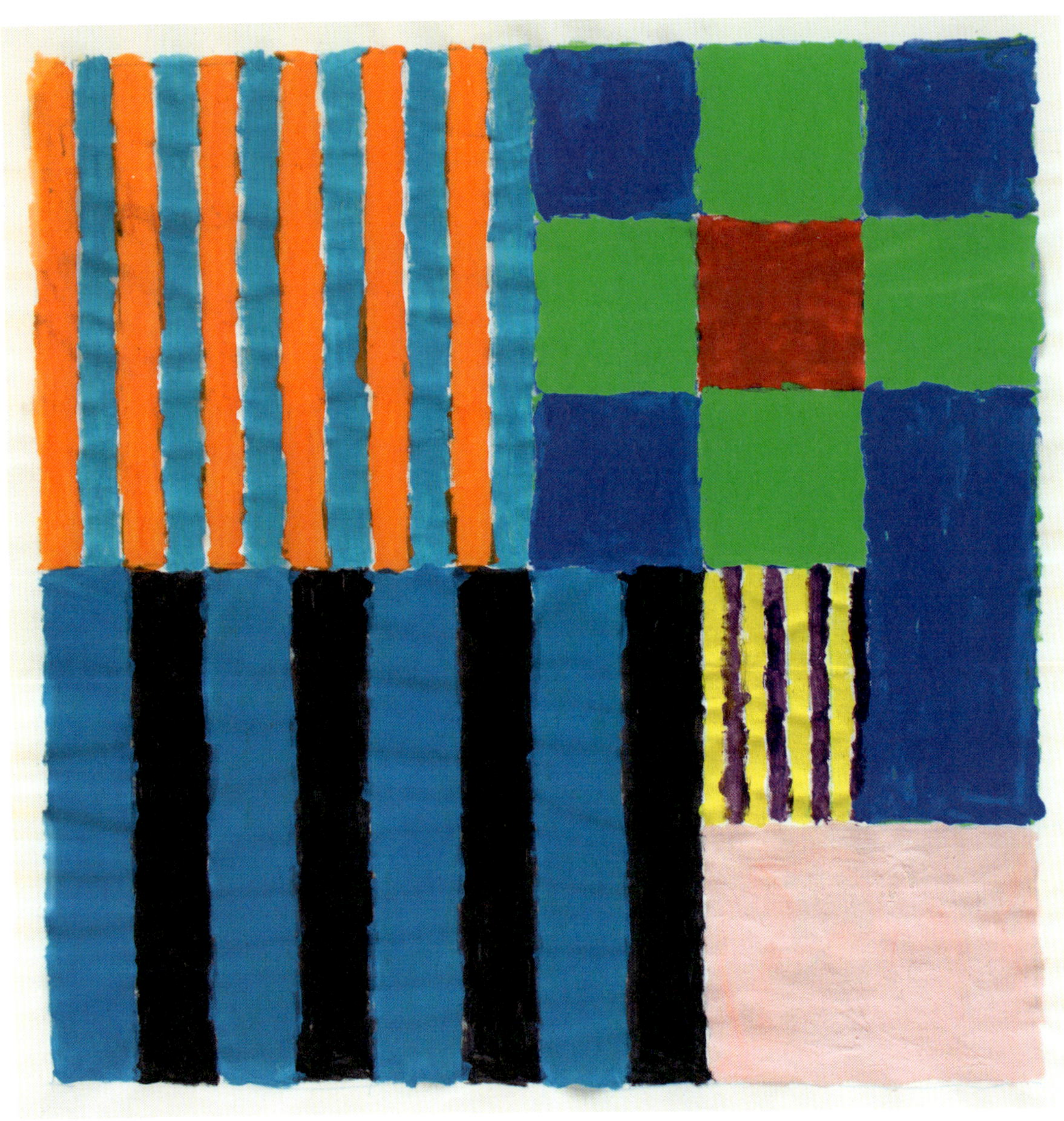

 Landscape with Tree, 1978, gouache and pencil on paper, 12 × 12 inches

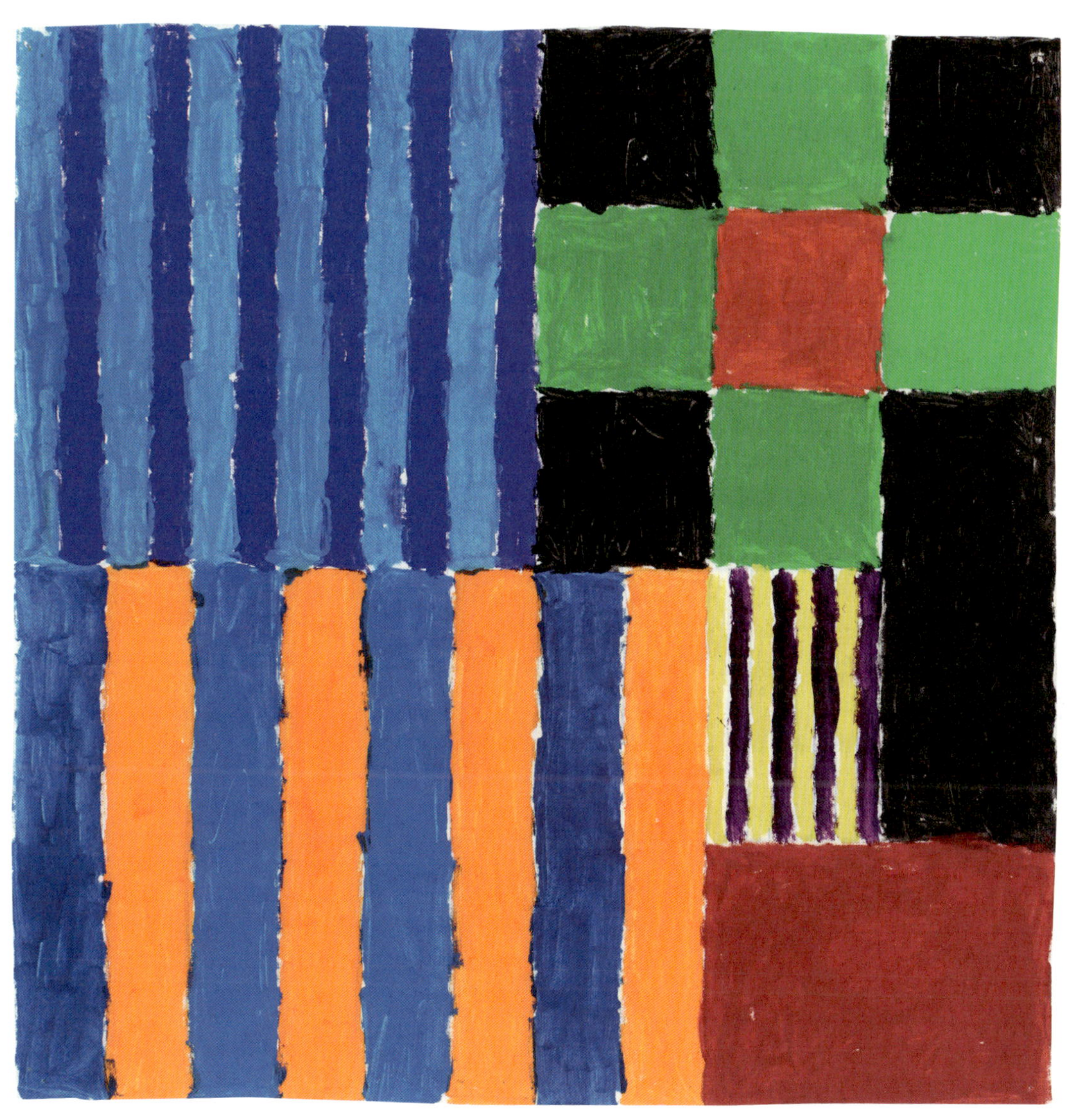

113 *Landscape with Tree*, 1978, gouache and pencil on paper, 12 × 12 inches

Crucifictions

 Crucifiction, 1978, gouache and pencil on paper, 11 × 4 inches

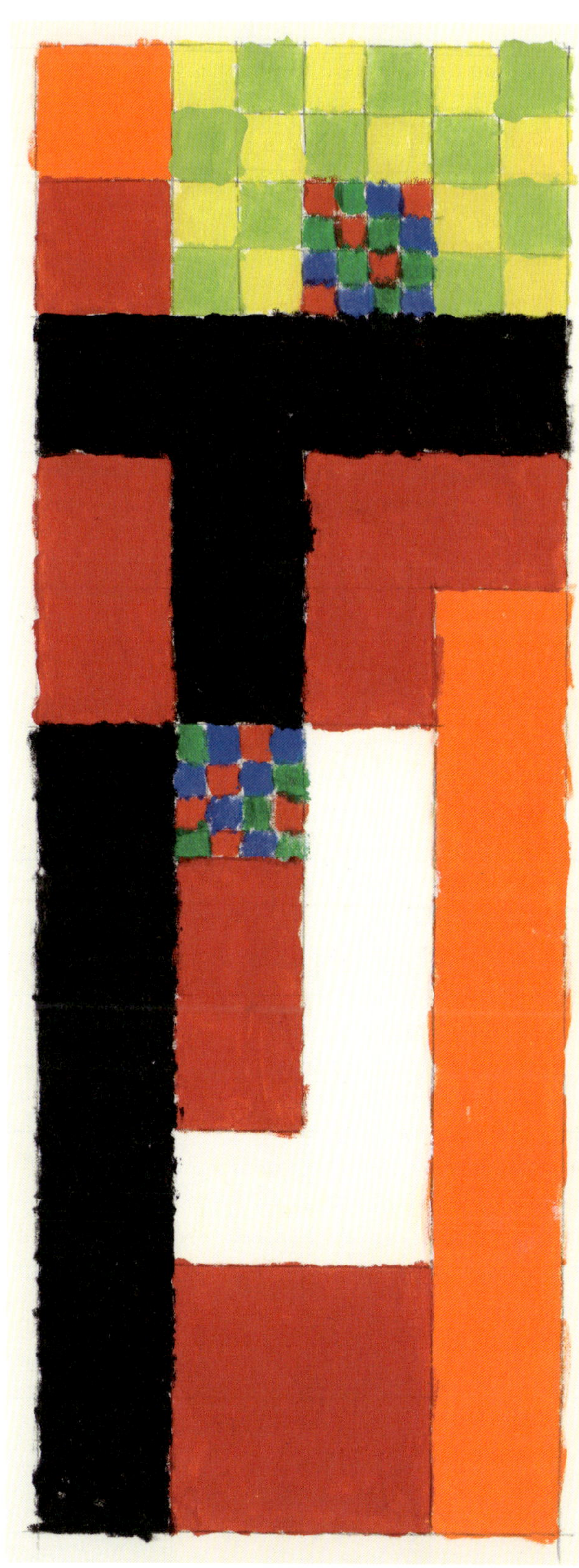

118 *Crucifiction*, 1978, gouache and pencil on paper, 15 × 8 inches

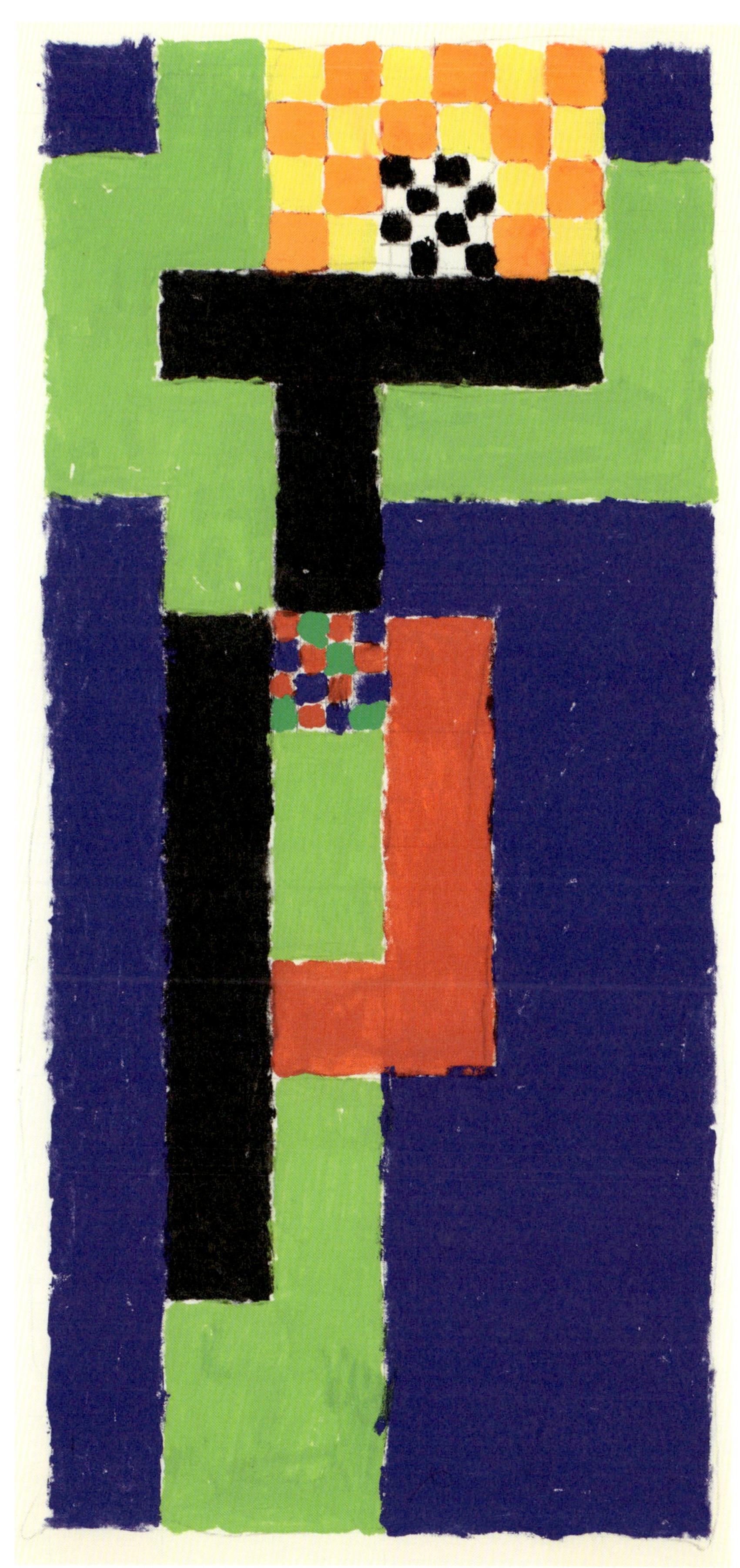

Figures

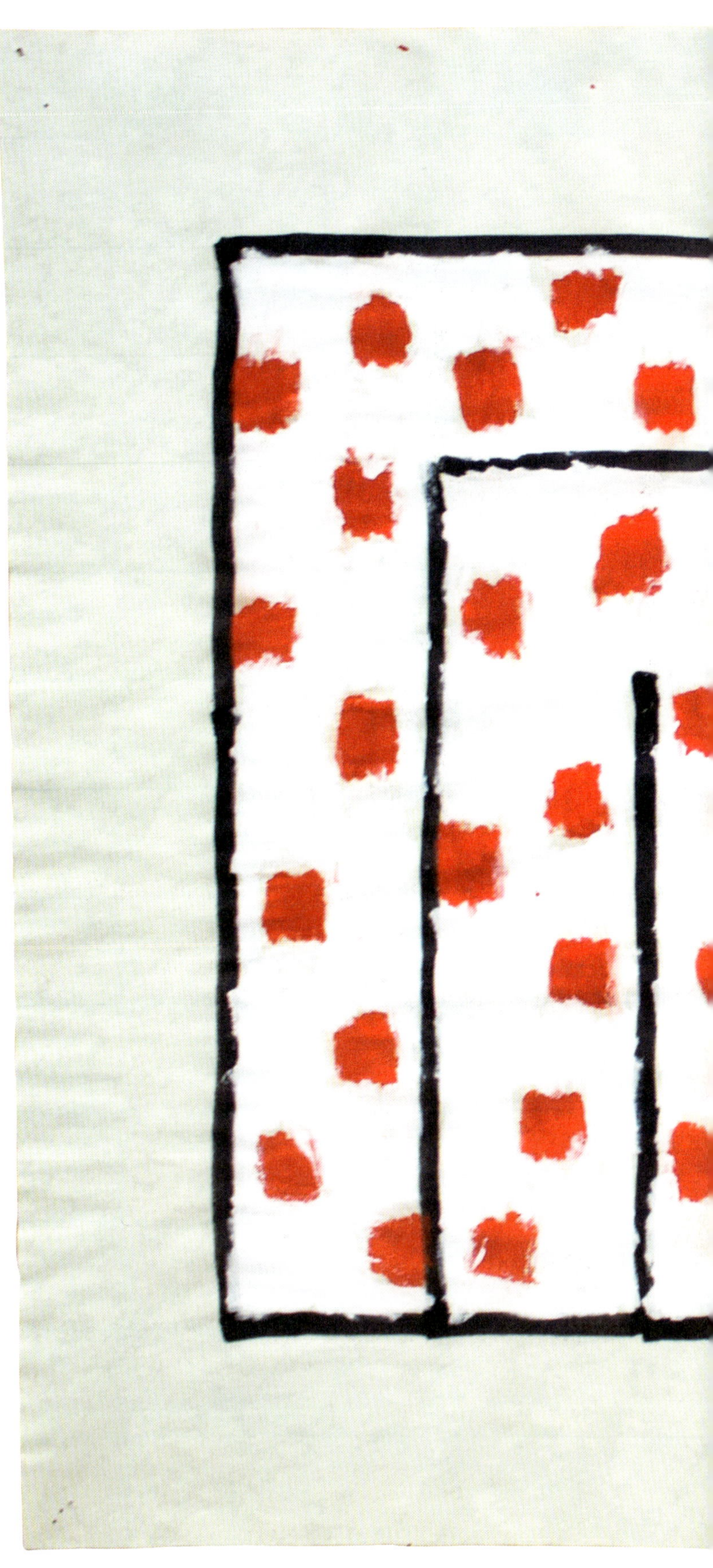

 Reclining Figure, 1977, gouache and marker on paper, 14 × 22 inches

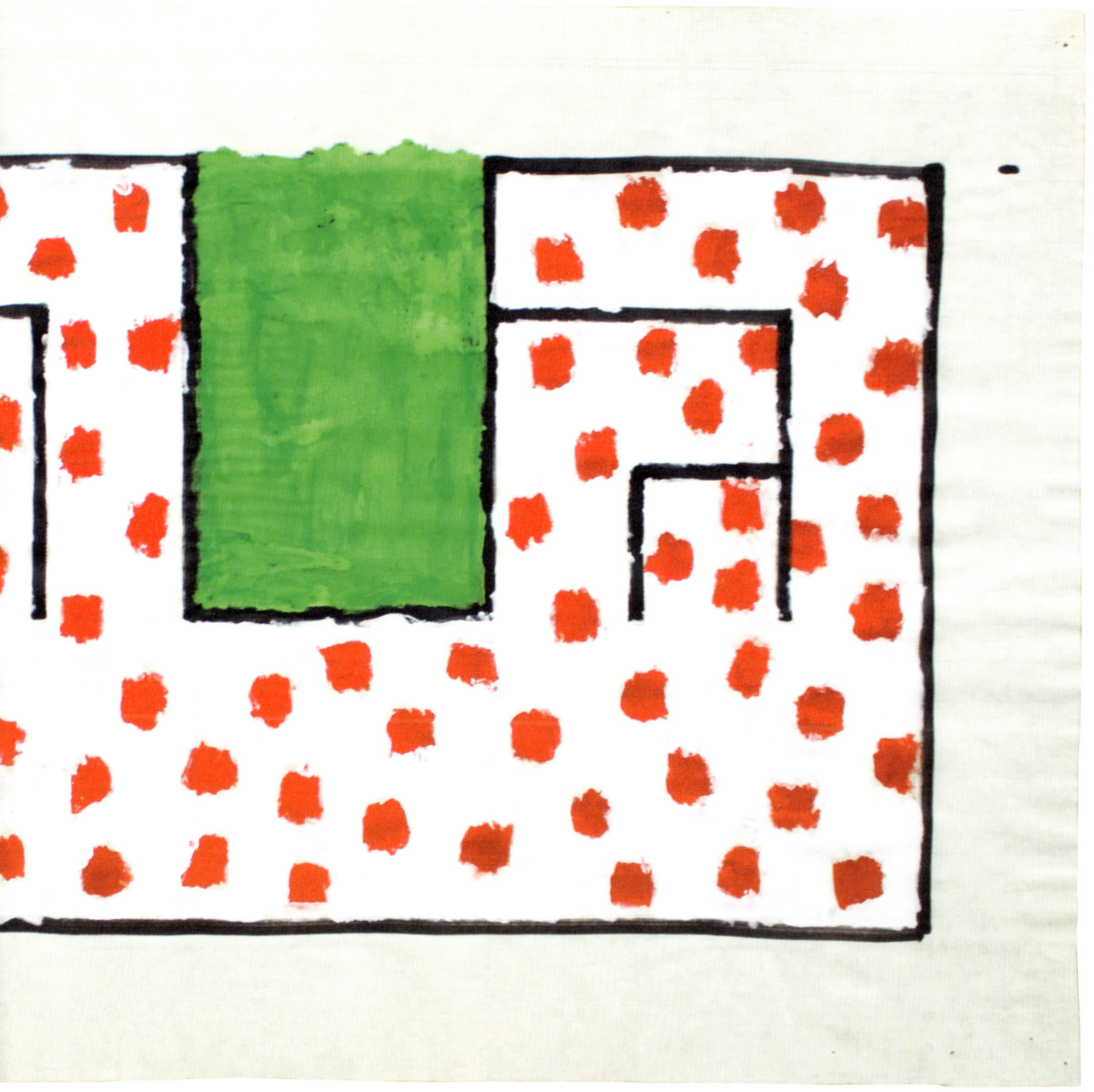

Sharay, 1978, gouache and pencil on paper, 6 × 7 inches

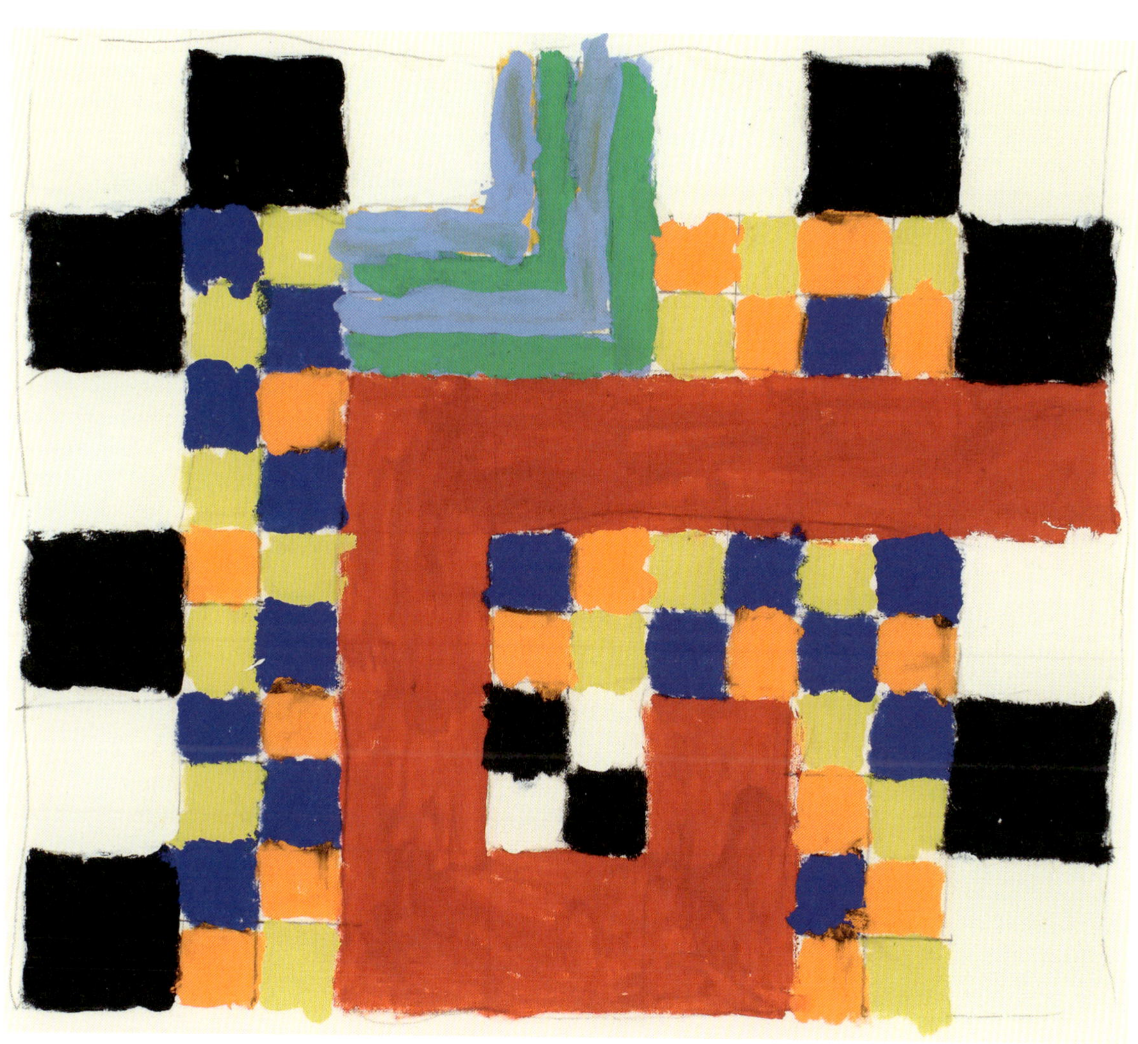

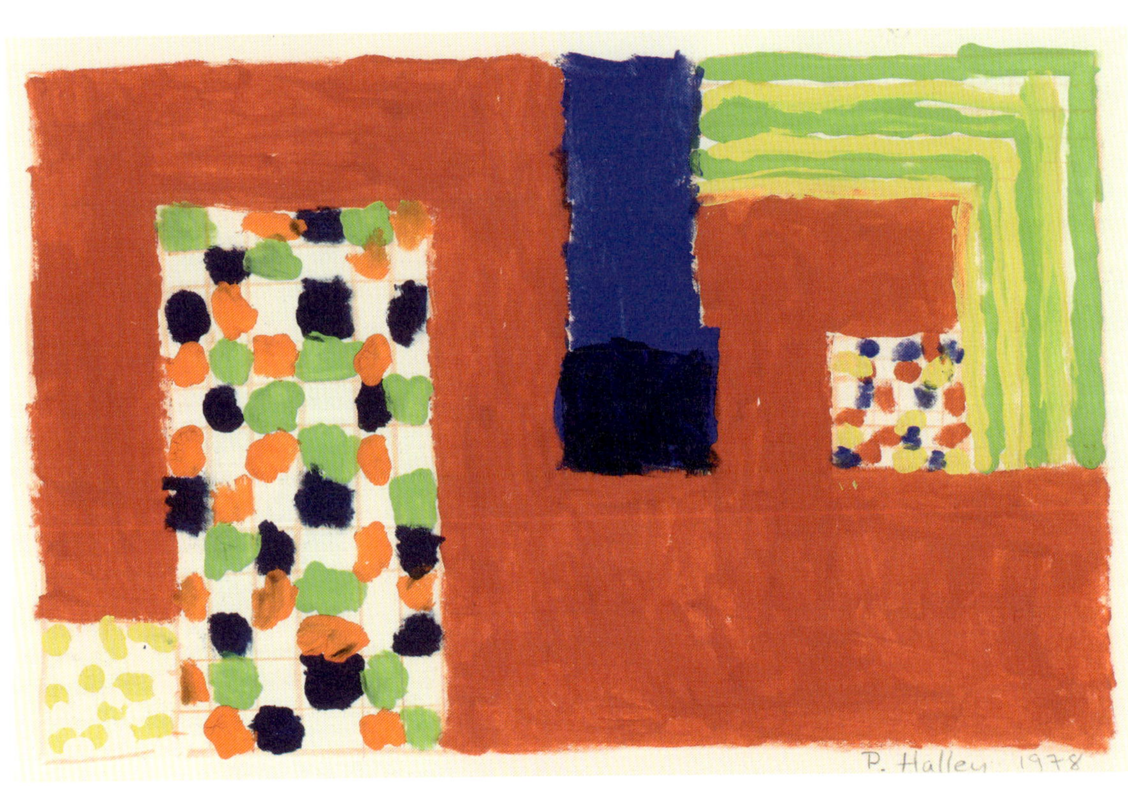

 Red Nude, 1978, gouache and pencil on paper, 5 × 8 inches

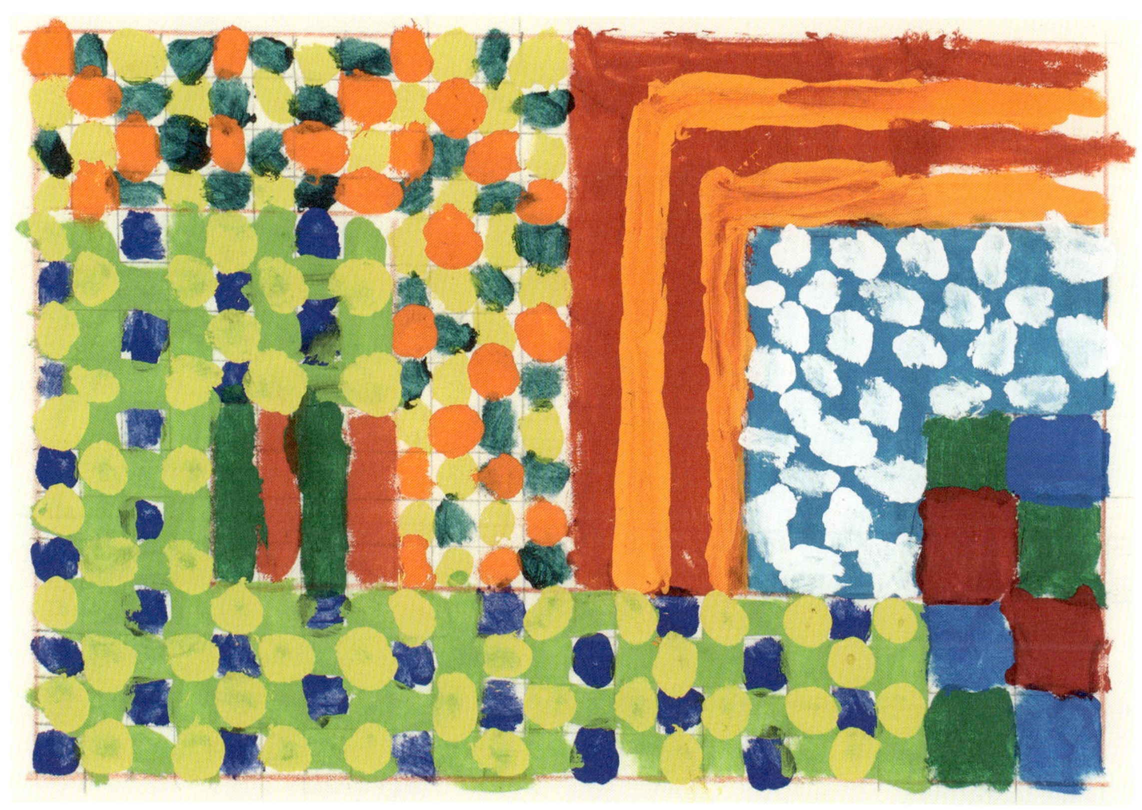

127 *Reclining Figure*, 1978, gouache and pencil on paper, 4 × 6 inches

A Japanese Woman Washing Her Hair, 1978, gouache and pencil on paper with collage element, 10 × 8 inches

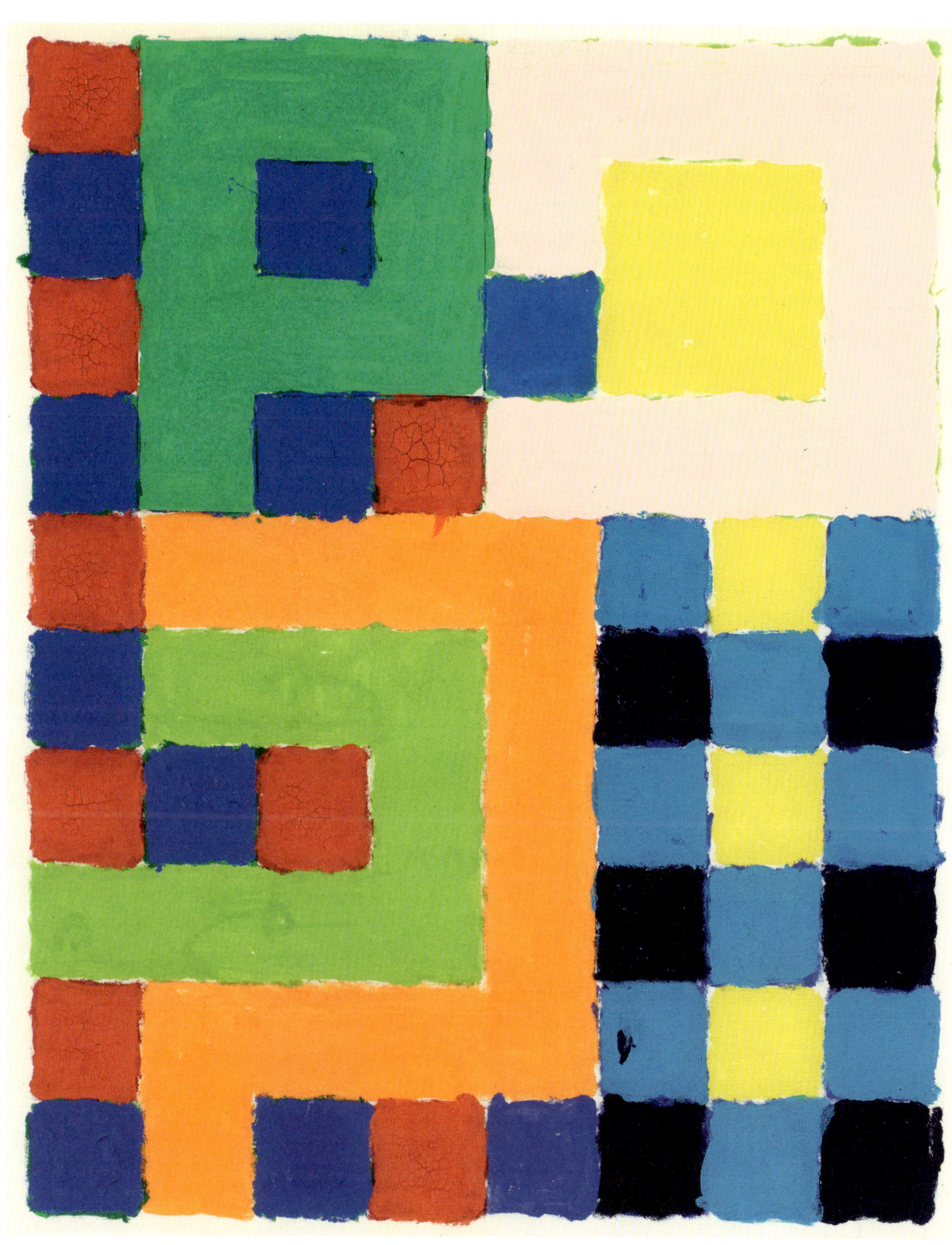

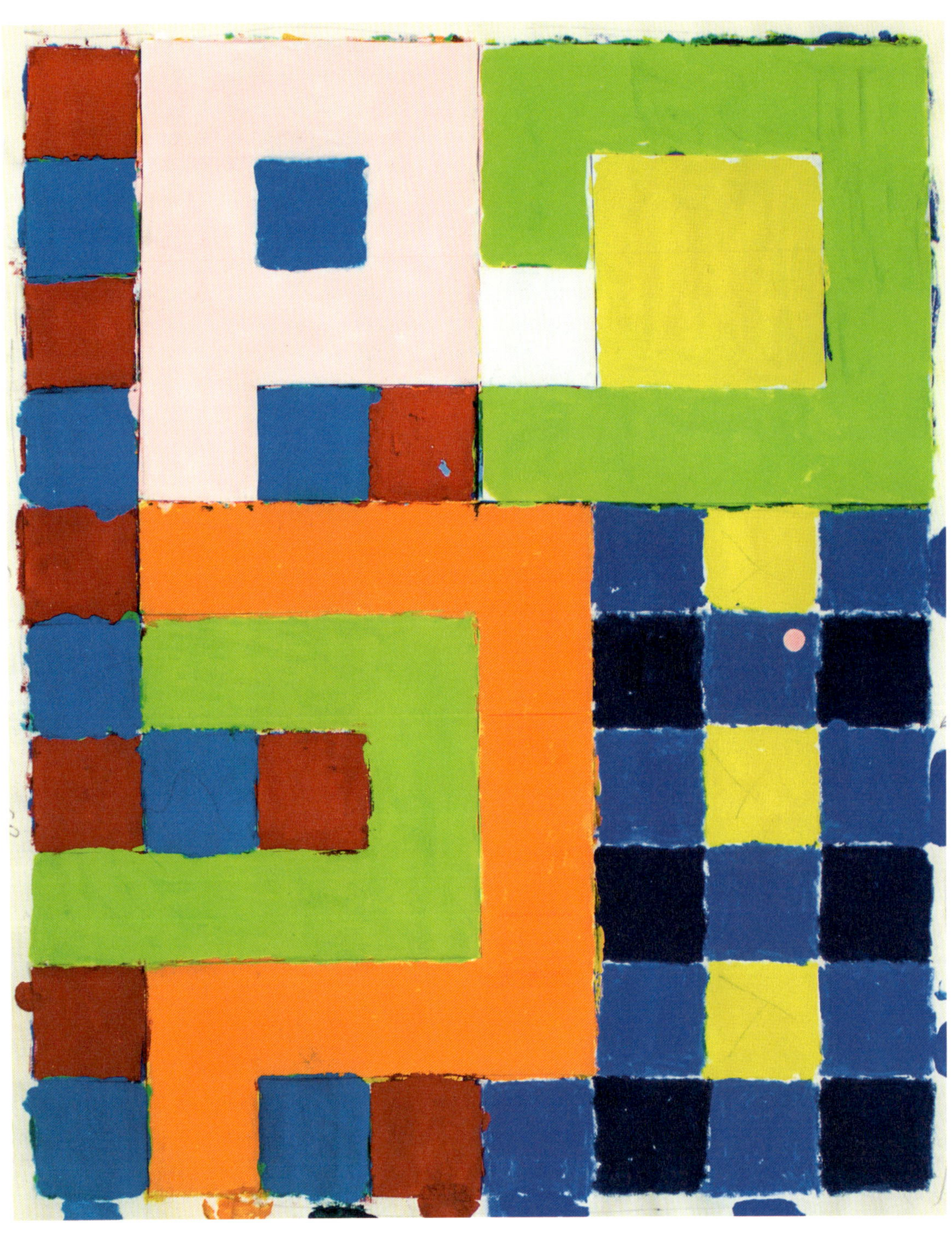

 A Japanese Woman Washing Her Hair, 1978, gouache and pencil on paper with collage element, 10 × 8 inches

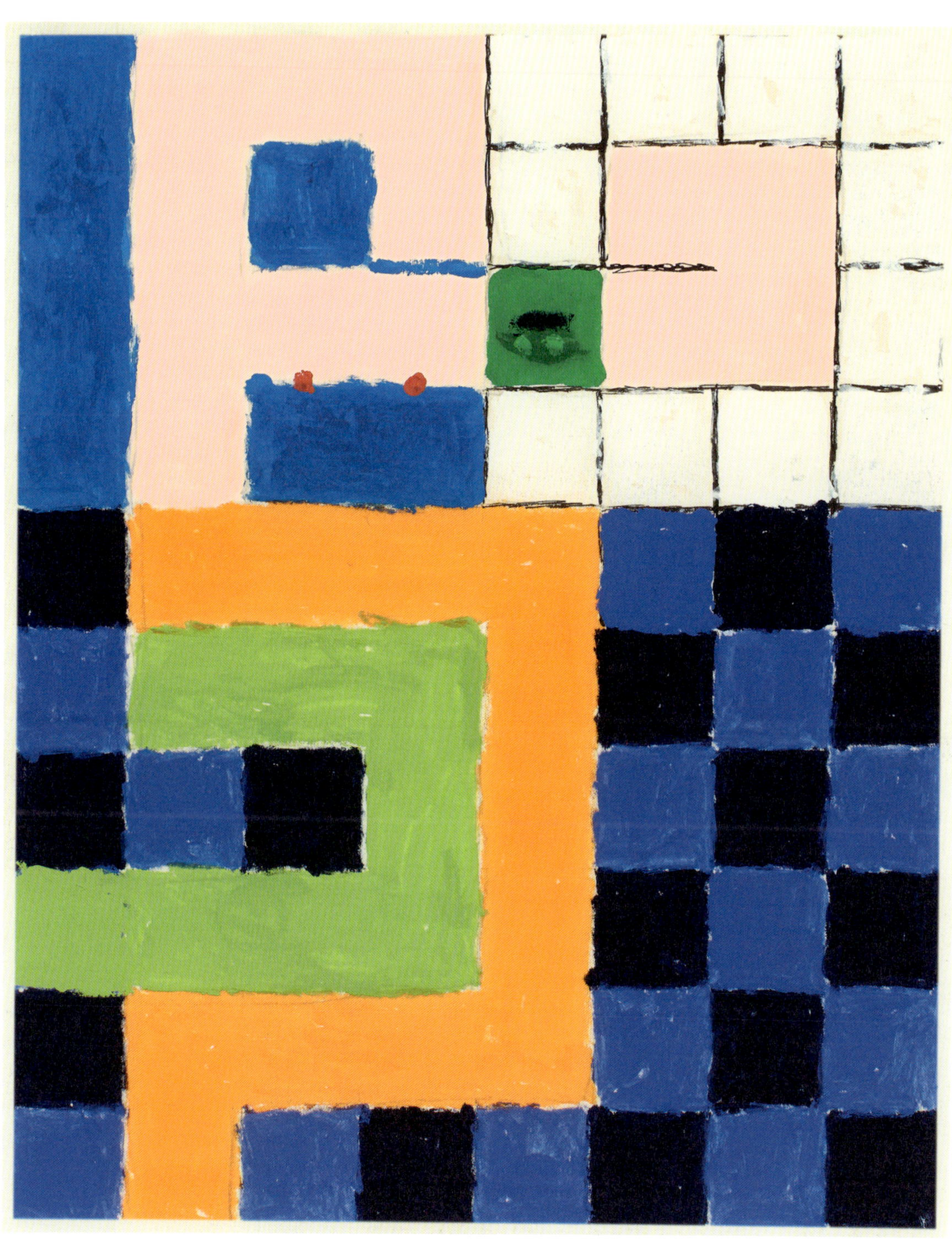

131 *A Japanese Woman Washing Her Hair*, 1978, gouache and marker on paper, 10 × 8 inches

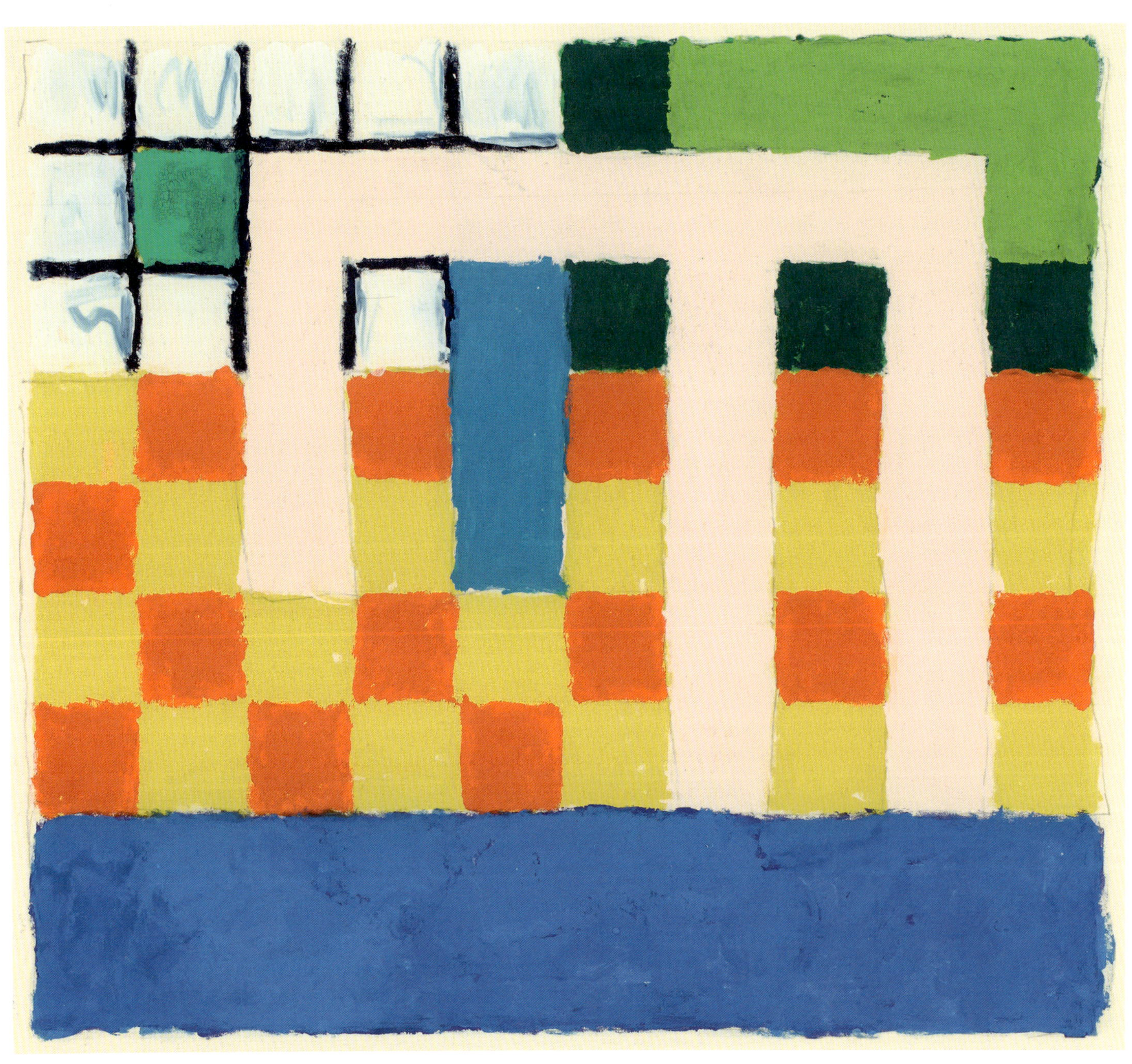

 Bathing Figure, 1978, gouache and pencil on paper, 11 × 12 inches

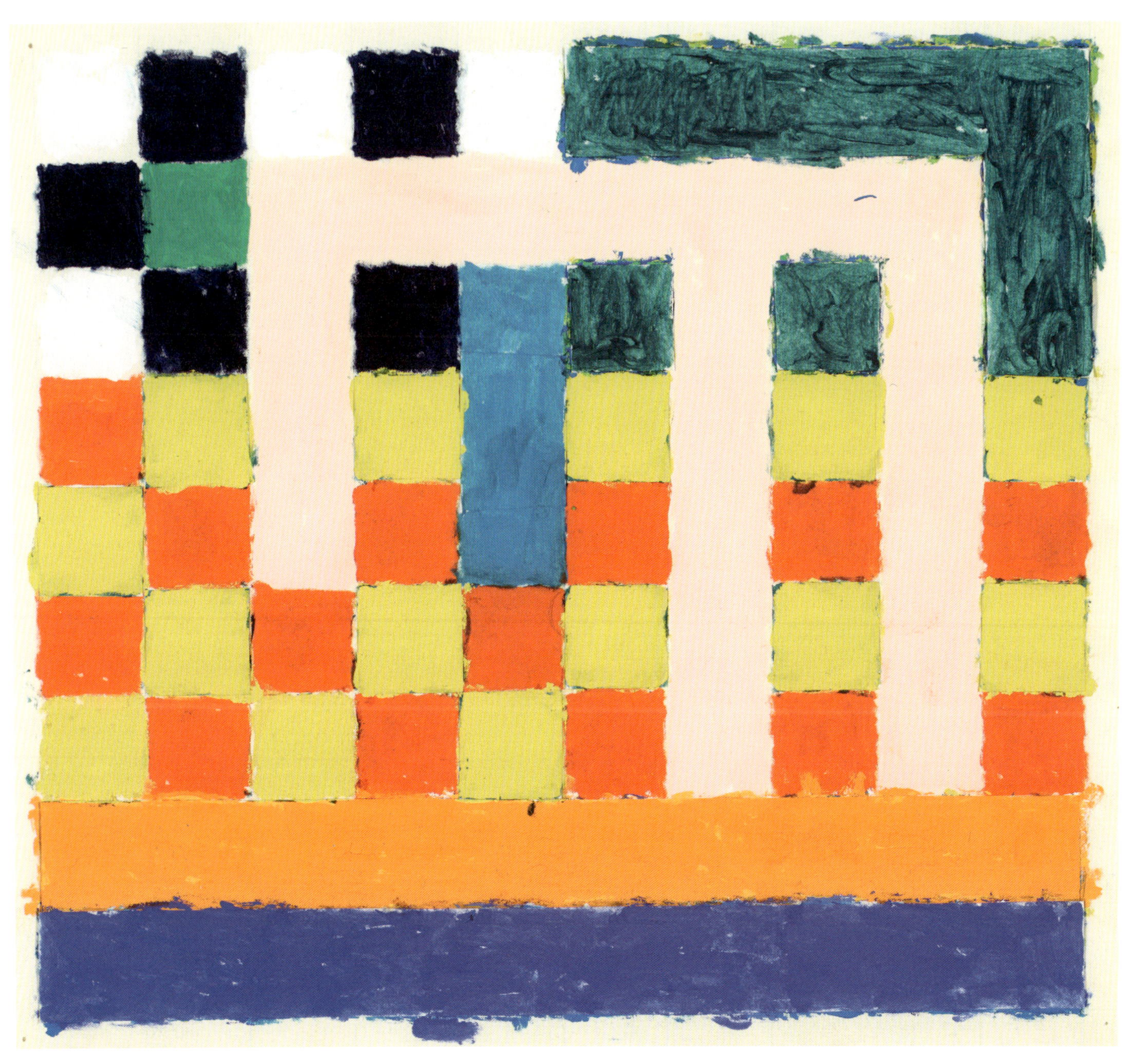

133 *Bathing Figure*, 1978, gouache and pencil on paper with collage element, 11 × 12 inches

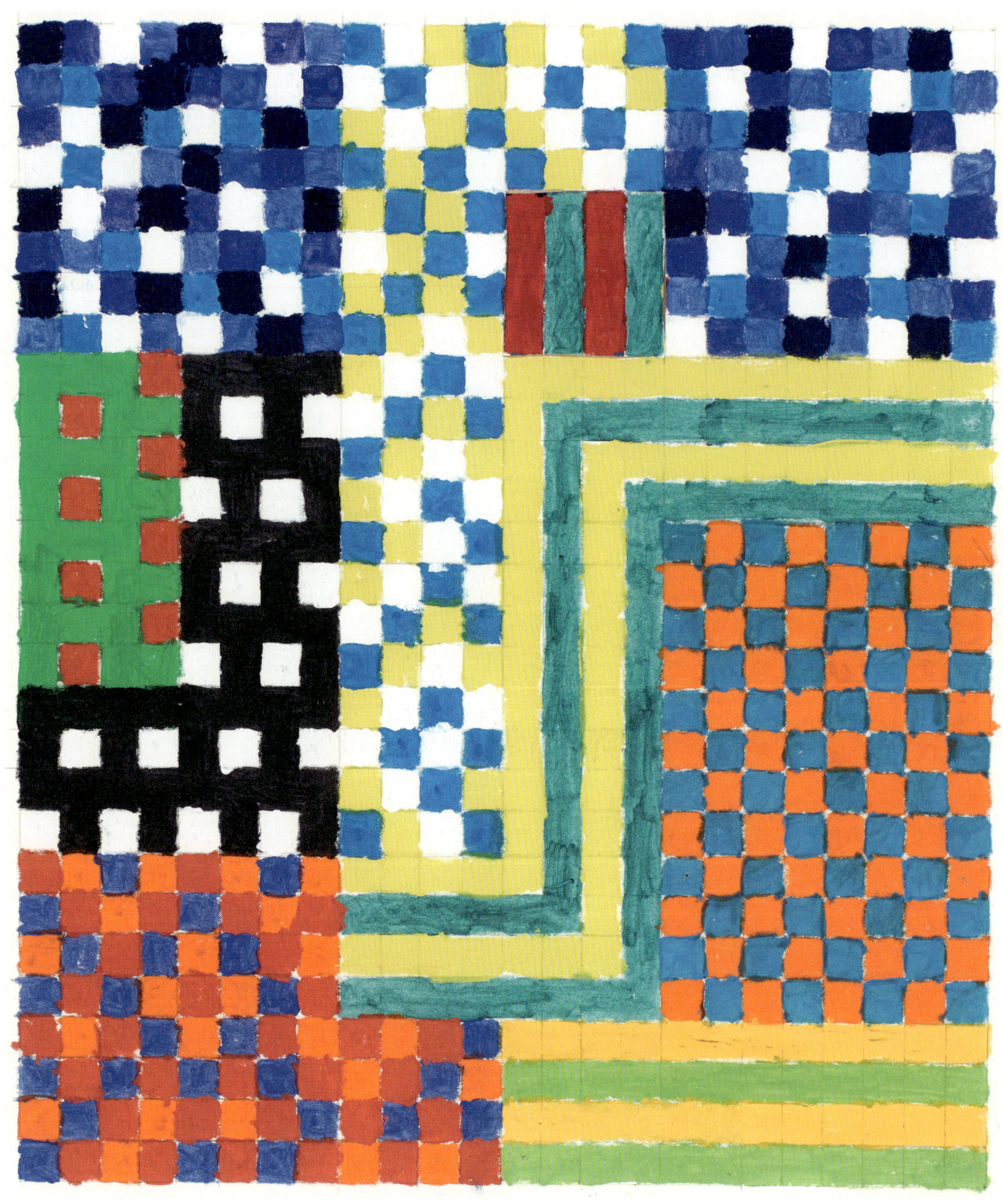

 Sharay I, 1978, gouache on paper, 16 × 14 inches

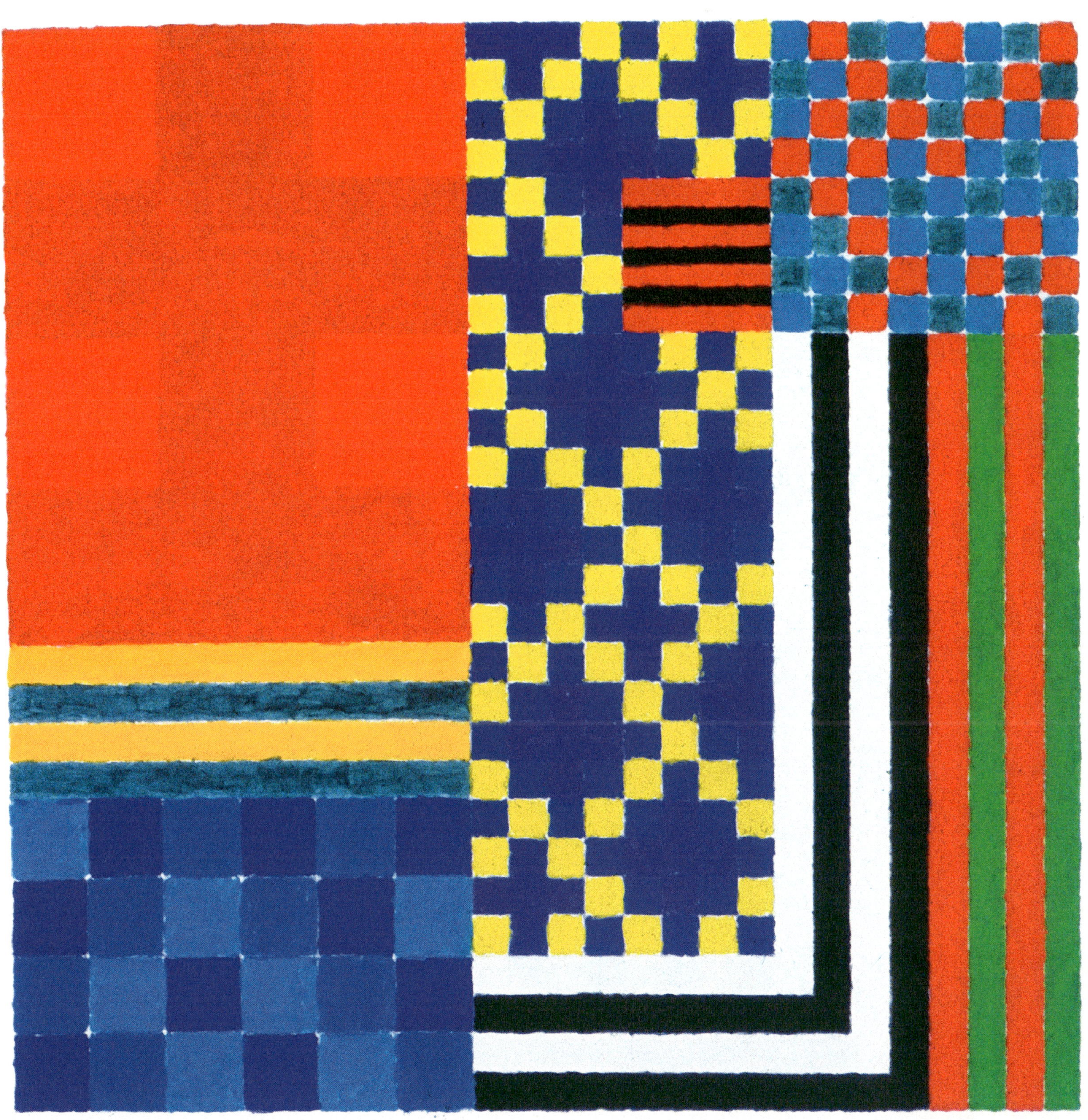

135 *Sharay II*, 1978, gouache and pencil on paper, 27 × 27 inches

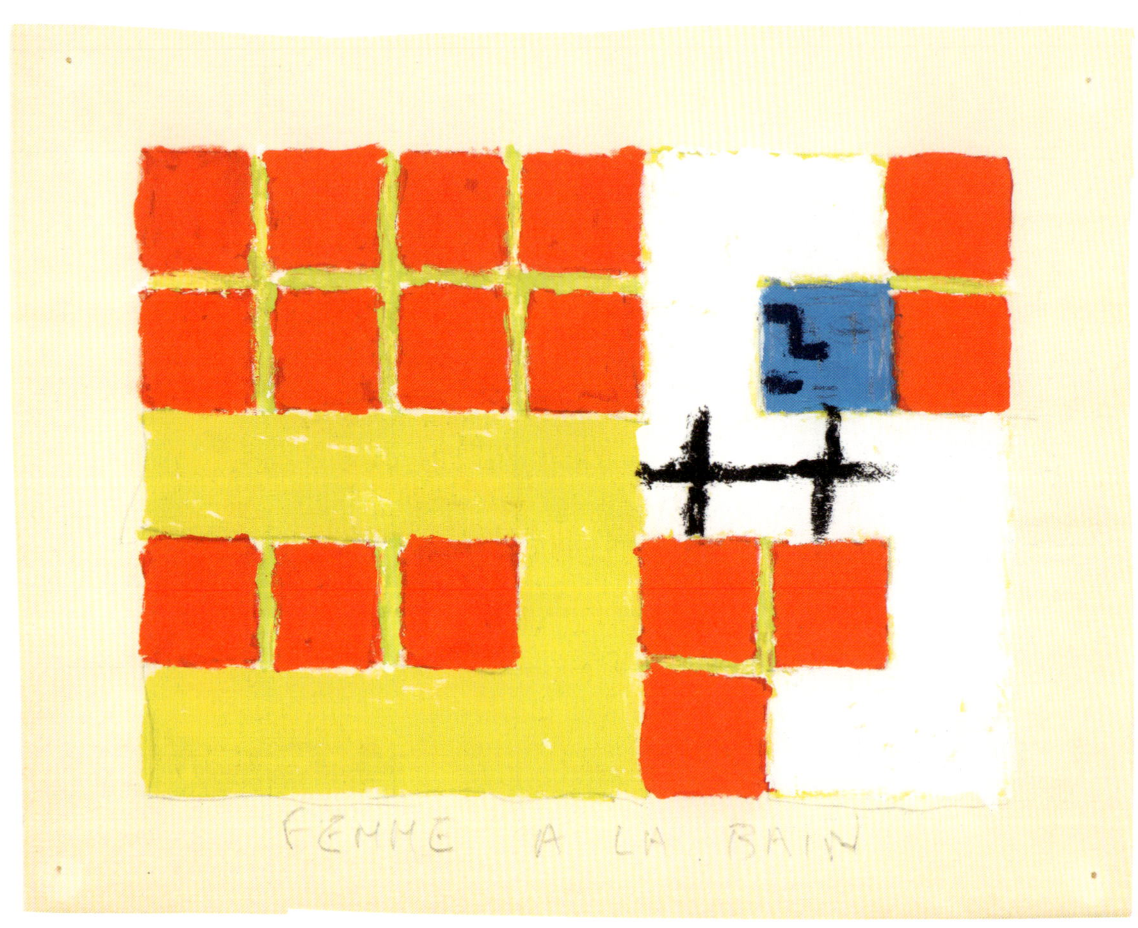

 Femme a la Bain, 1978, gouache and pencil on paper, 7 × 9 inches

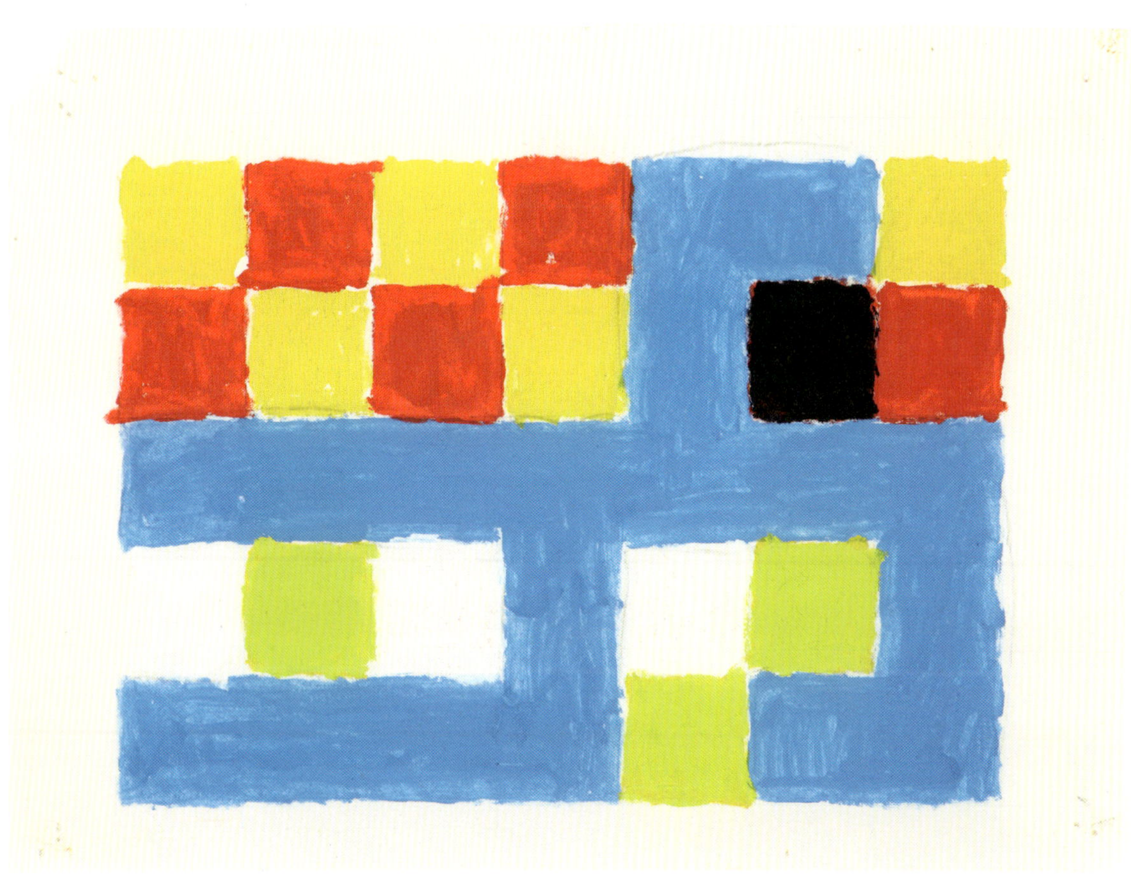

137 *Femme a la Bain, 1978*, gouache and pencil on paper, 6½ × 9 inches

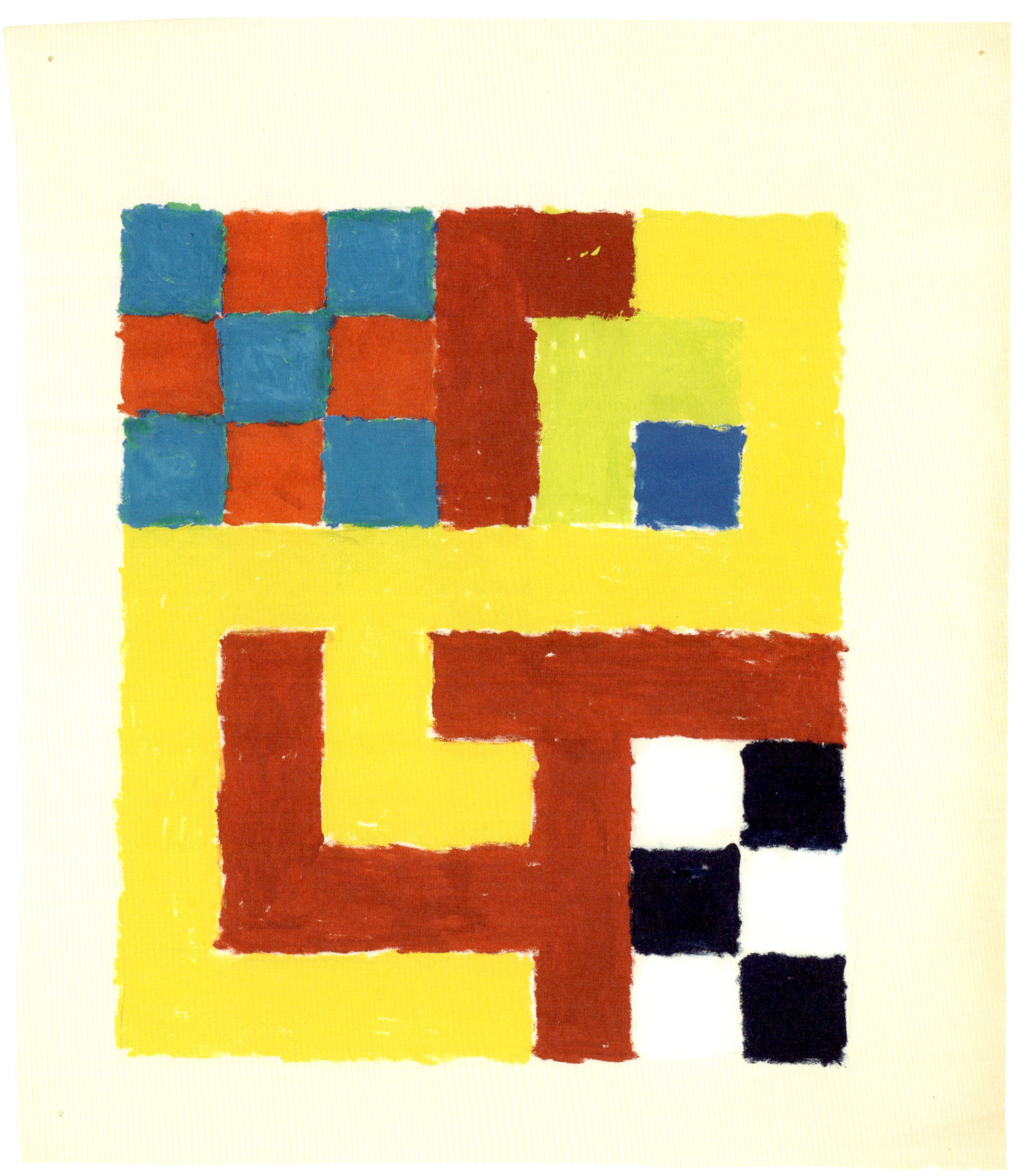

 Femme Couchée, 1978, gouache and pencil on paper, 11 × 9½ inches

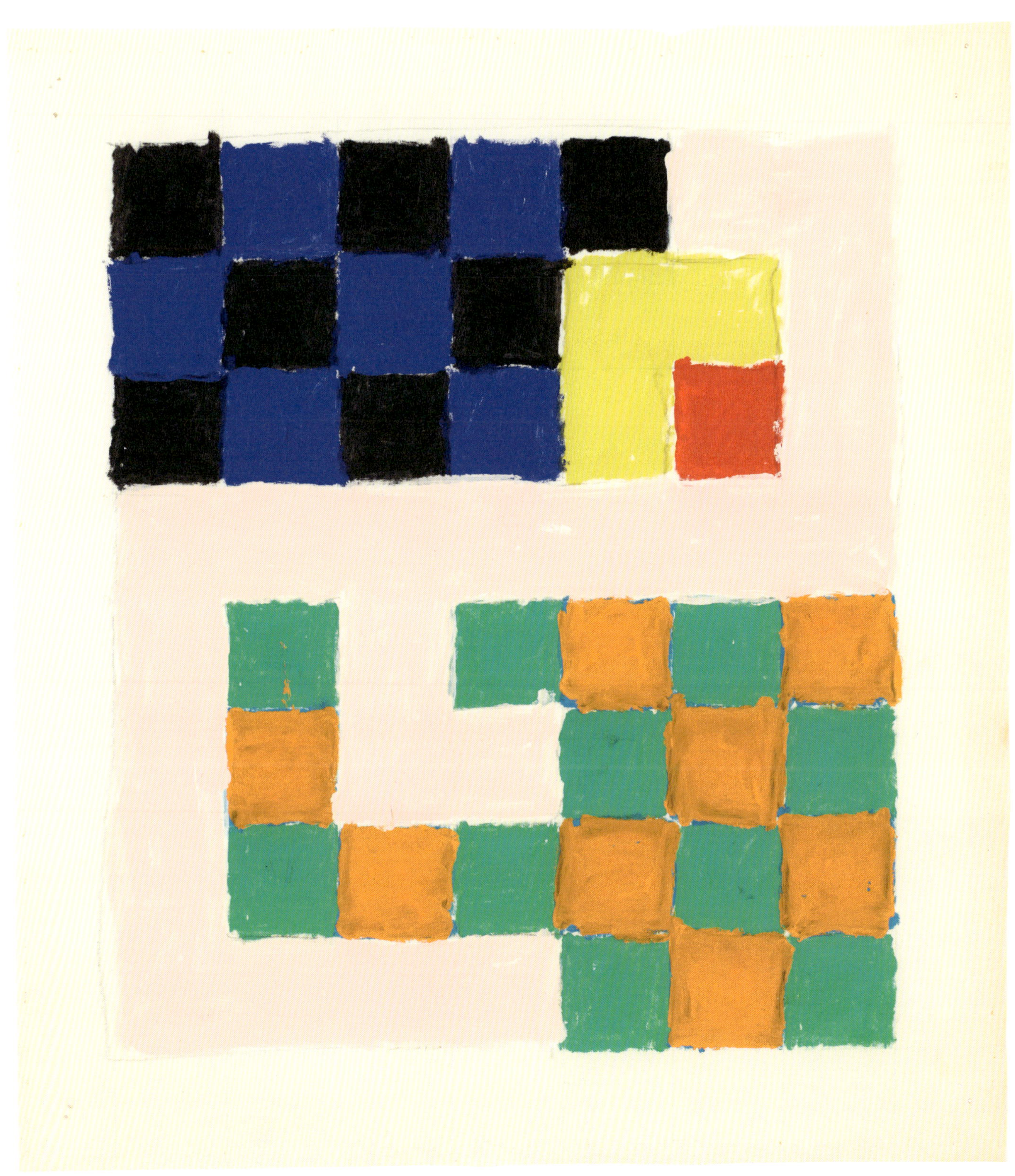

139 *Femme Couchée*, 1978, gouache and pencil on paper, 10 × 9 inches

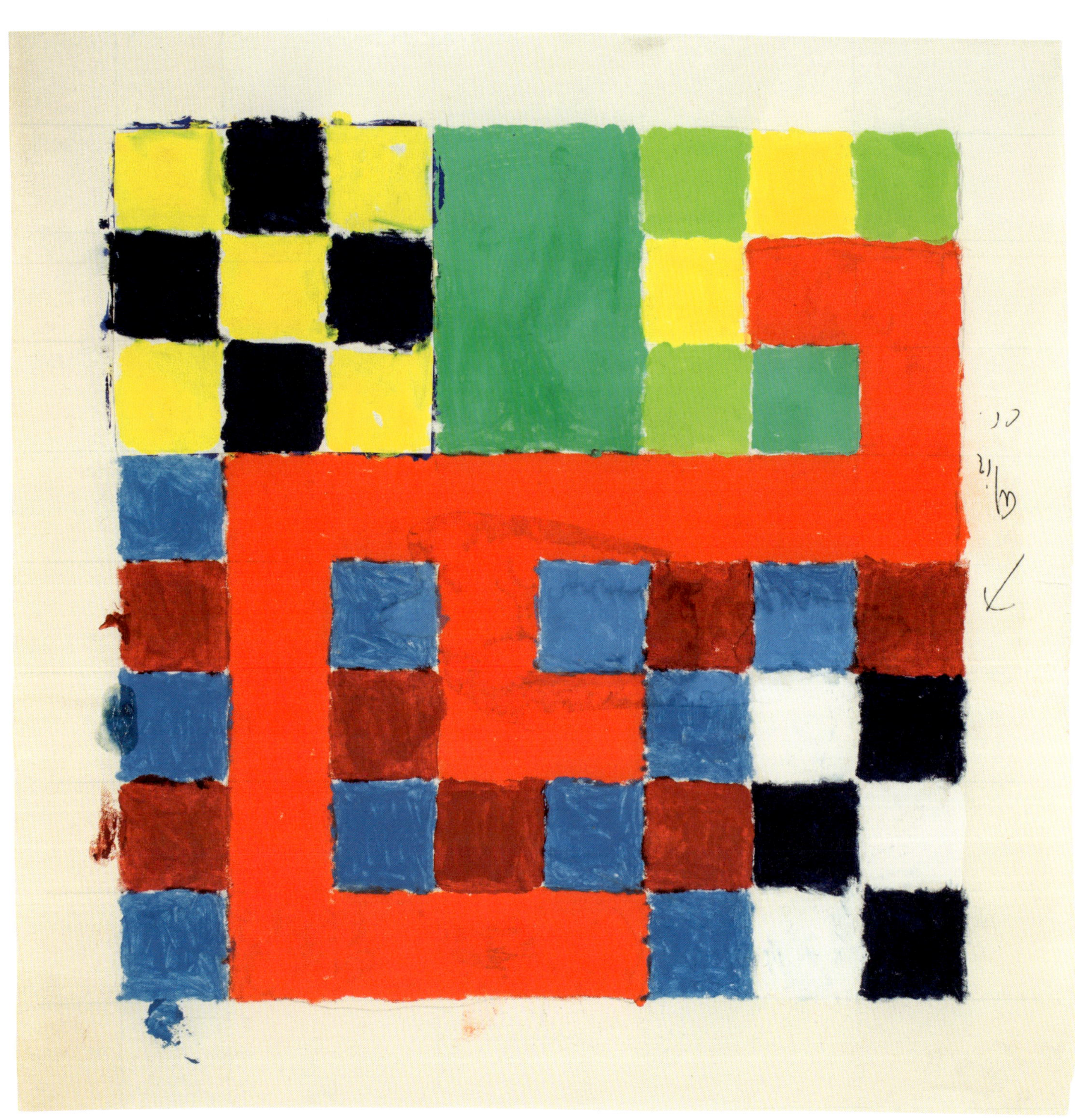

140 *Femme Couchée*, 1978, gouache and pencil on paper with collage element, 10 × 10 inches

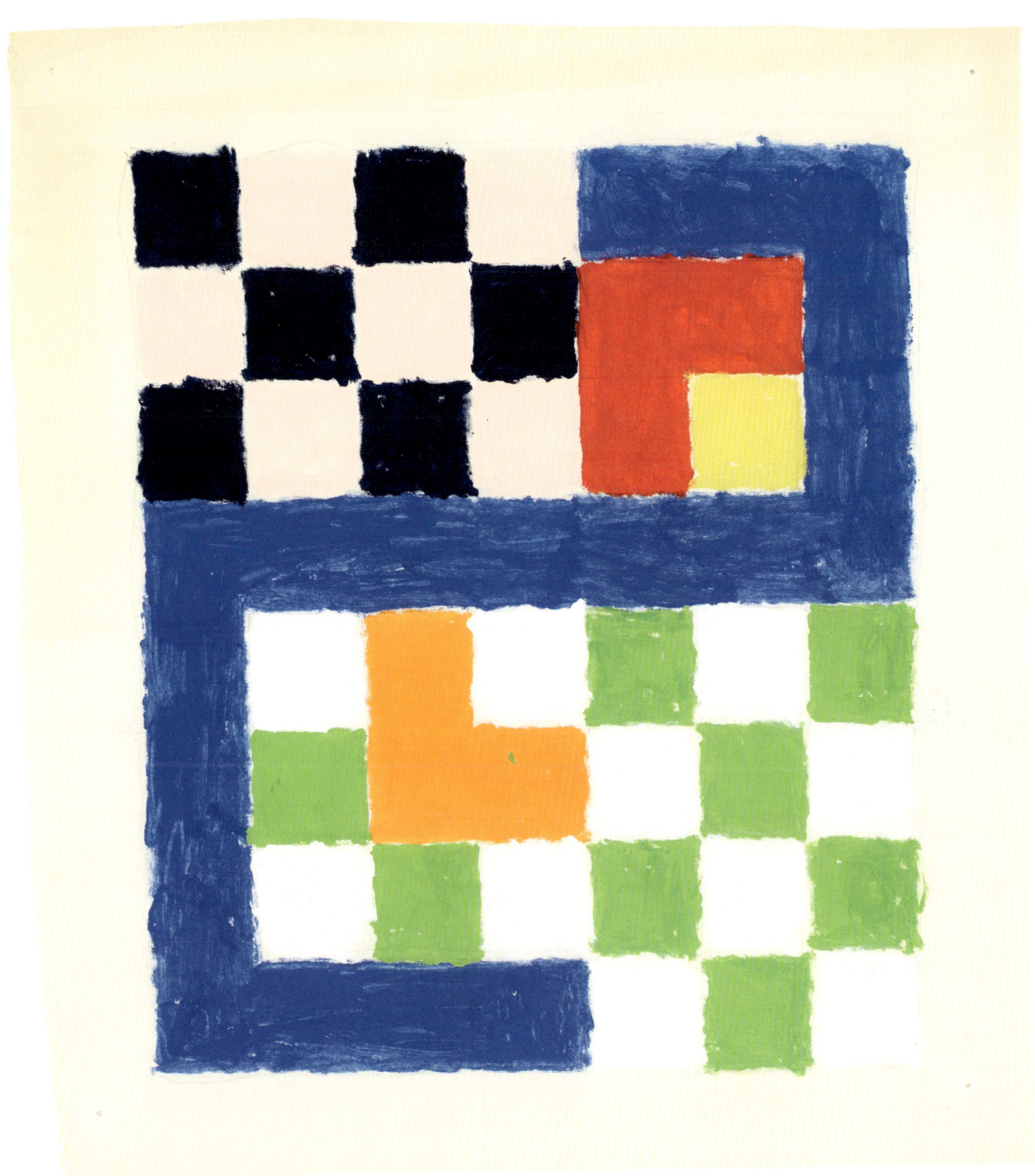

141 *Femme Couchée*, 1978, gouache and pencil on paper, 10 × 9 inches

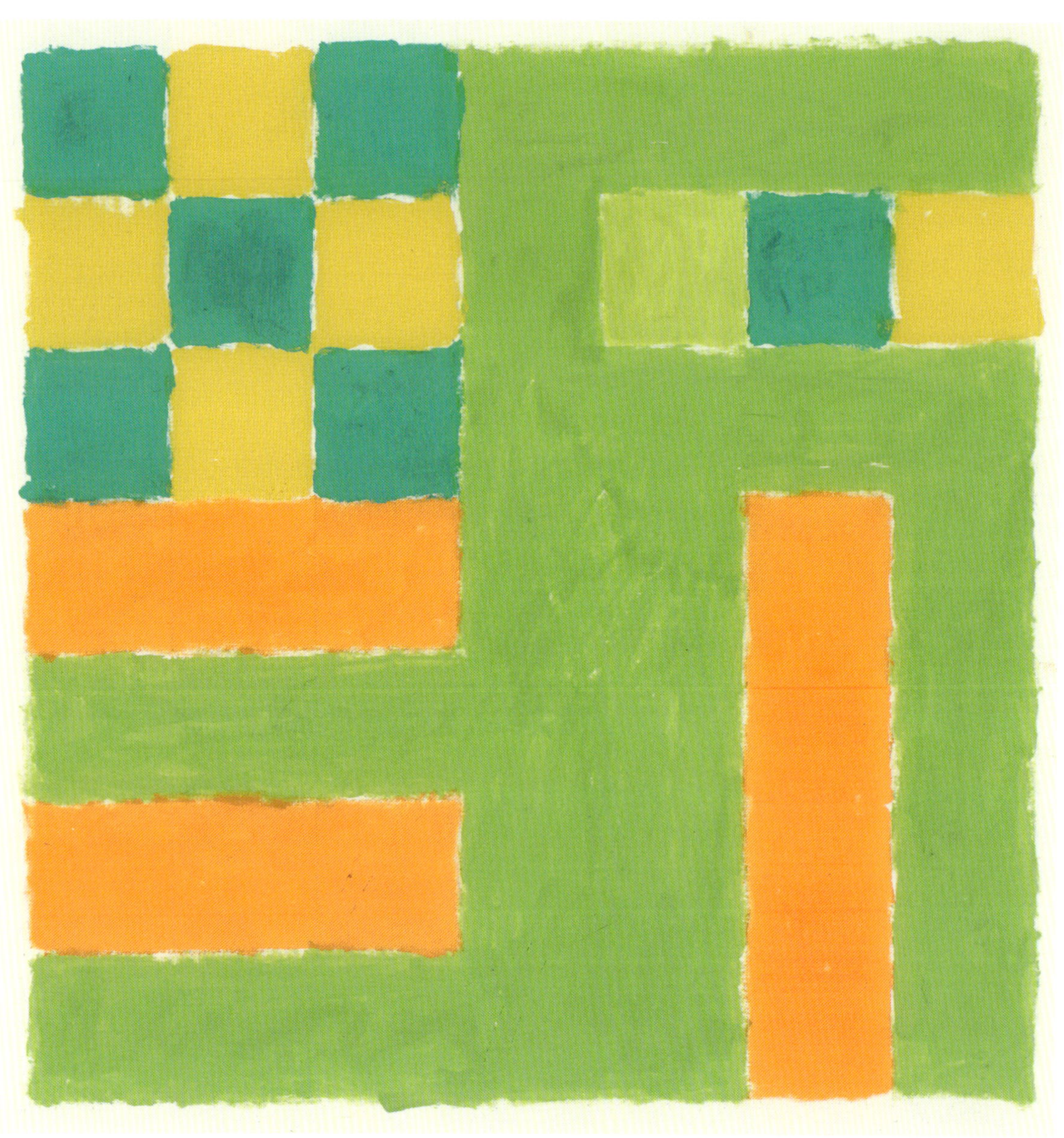

 Seated Figure, 1978, gouache and pencil on paper, 7 × 7 inches

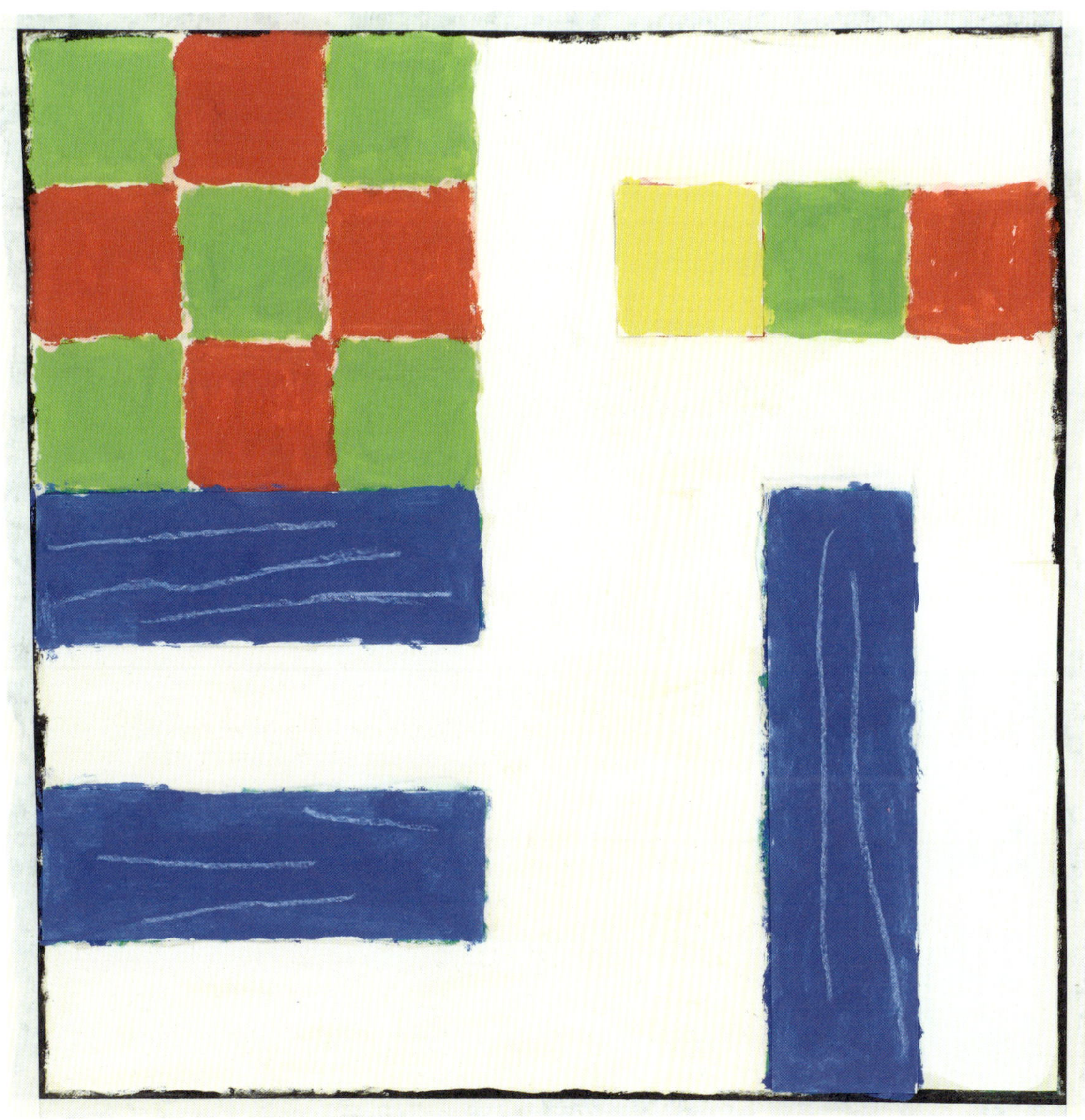

143 *Seated Figure*, 1978, gouache and pencil on paper, 7 × 7 inches

Peter Halley
Boats Crosses Trees Figures 1977–78

Published on the occasion
of the exhibition at

Karma
188 E 2nd Street
New York, NY 10009
March 1–31, 2017

Edition of 1500
Special edition of 100

ISBN: 978-1-942607-62-5